TELL ME HOW LONG YOU WANT TO LIVE
TO LIVE
AND I'LL TELL YOU WHAT TO
EAT TO GET THERE

By

Dr. William D. Stimack

and

Barbara Rolek

ISBN: 0-7596-8213-5

This book is printed on acid free paper.

1stBooks - rev. 01/22/02

DEDICATIONS

I dedicate this book with love to the most wonderful, caring, beautiful, kind, reverent, fun wife of 37 years, my precious Jean.

William D. Stimack

I dedicate this work to my parents and to everyone who has ever searched for some small measure of relief, if not a cure, from a chronic, debilitating illness. Food may very well be the only medicine we need.

Barbara Rolek

CONTENTS

ix

FOREWORD

As an educator, I recognize the value of good resources for the purpose of educating those who are seeking wellness through natural means. This book provides forthright evidence of the significance of good nutrition and proper lifestyle. Dr. Stimack's extensive knowledge and experience as a naturopathic physician really shine through.

In Dr. Stimack's and Ms. Rolek's book, we are reminded that the present condition of our bodies is literally the result of what we think, feel and eat. They have provided us with a valuable resource that will not only benefit the patient but practitioner alike. Knowing what foods are good for us is one thing, being able to apply this knowledge in our day-to-day lives is another. The authors' thoughtful inclusion of food preparation guides and recipes enables you to make decisions about your health that will positively change your life.

I first had the pleasure of becoming acquainted with Dr. Stimack when he attended Southern College of Naturopathic Medicine where I serve as president. I am very proud of his accomplishments and I admire his commitment to natural medicine. I will certainly recommend this book to my colleagues, friends and family.

Gary Axley, O.M.D., N.M.D.

Tell Me How Long You Want to Live and I'll Tell You What to Eat to Get There is a book on nutrition no home should be without. Dr. Stimack and Ms. Rolek explore a simple but profound concept—"You are what you eat." All disease is cellular and all nutrients either positively or negatively affect the cell. This is a scientifically sound book, yet not beyond the understanding of the novice seeking solutions for maximum health and self-determination.

William Washington, M.D., Internal Medicine Specialist

ACKNOWLEDGMENTS

Dr. Stimack wishes to gratefully acknowledge the following:

My father, who now lives with God, for instilling in me a work ethic and giving me the rules of life.

My mother, who is still here, for urging and supporting me in everything I do.

My sister, Kathy Robinson, who is the greatest sister in the world.

My niece, Janet Fernandez, who always believed in her Uncle Bill.

Dr. Gary Axley, who is a good friend, a good Marine, and a great doctor. He showed me not only was I a doctor, but a damned good one.

Martin A. Berns, who spreads integrity, loyalty, honesty, and a sense of fair play in everything and every person he touches.

Howard Levine, who is the most brilliant man I have ever met.

Dr. Jack Price, a man's man. If you are ever in a foxhole, you need to hope he's in there with you.

Roane Follis, who has shown me what hope, trust and belief can do.

Shirley Williams, Bob Able, Judy Follis, Joyce Miller, Steven Seigel, Valerie Thill and James Williams for their unfailing help.

My children John and Michael House, and little Jeannie, who is now 28 years old but will always be Daddy's Little Girl.

And last, but not least, God Almighty. If it were not for God's love, understanding and forgiveness, none of this would be possible.

To all of you, remember, God loves you and so do I.

Barbara Rolek would like to acknowledge the following:

Shirley Williams for making sure Dr. Stimack and I crossed paths.

April Metz for her invaluable research assistance.

Marie Oser for blazing a trail in her bestsellers, *Soy of Cooking* and *More Soy Cooking.*

Cathy Thomas of the *Orange County Register* for her educational food articles.

Jean Stimack, Judy Follis, Shirley and James Williams, and Branka Kojic for their recipes.

My mother and father for instilling a love of words in me and for providing the education I needed to put them together.

My sister who has always believed in me, even when I doubted myself.

My brother and sister-in-law for their love and humor.

My culinary associates, past and present, for sharing their knowledge.

INTRODUCTION

I had a career in sales, marketing and consulting for many years, and I was very successful. But when members of my family became ill and weren't getting the results we had hoped for with conventional treatment, I set out to learn all I could about complementary and alternative medicine, or, as I prefer to call it, integrated medicine.

My quest for knowledge resulted in a doctorate of naturopathy and a doctorate of naturopathic medicine from Southern College of Naturopathy in Boles, Arkansas. I'm proud to say that while I was in school I paid attention; I maintained a 4.0 gradepoint average for a total of 156 credits and 1,202 clinical hours of study.

So what is a naturopath? A naturopath is a practitioner who believes in the healing powers of nature and uses integrated medical practices—proper nutrition, herbal remedies, prayer, massage therapy, meditation, visualization, acupuncture—along with modern scientific diagnostic methods and standards of care in treating illnesses.

To remain current in the field, I attend conferences and seminars on a regular basis and was lucky enough to meet the Dalai Lama who headed the First Tibetan Medical Convention in Washington, D.C., in 2000. That was quite an experience.

Another was the Comprehensive Cancer Care conference held in Washington, D.C., also in 2000, sponsored by the University of Texas Medical School and the National Cancer Institute. It was amazing to see and hear about the alternative therapies being researched in the United States, especially the enzyme and visualization therapies for cancer that have met with much success.

The Office of Alternative Medicine (OAM) of the National Institutes of Health was established in 1992 by Congress to facilitate the fair, scientific evaluation of alternative therapies, and to reduce barriers that might keep them from gaining widespread use.

At that time, the OAM was allotted a budget of $1 million. In 2000, just eight short years later, it received 100 times that amount with funding of $100 million. Clearly, the government recognizes the efficacy of integrated medicine. Its time has come.

The more research I do on battling cancer and restoring health through nutrition, the more passionate and the more convinced I become that integrated medicine holds the most promise.

William D. Stimack, N.D., N.M.D.

I was a healthy foods skeptic. As a former executive chef with training in classic French techniques, a week without at least one meal laden with heavy cream was unimaginable to me!

It took reaching my bottom physically to discover that what I ate could make or break me, that food could be my medicine.

I have several autoimmune diseases—lupus, Sjogren's syndrome, fibromyalgia, Raynaud's disease—diabetes and sleep apnea. This cocktail of health disorders left me chronically exhausted and depressed.

The dominoes tumbled this way—the more tired I became, the less I did; the less I did, the more weight I gained; the more weight I gained, the worse my diabetes, sleep apnea and joint pain became; the worse my diabetes, sleep apnea and joint pain became, the more tired I was... It was a vicious cycle that caused a lot of guilt. "This must be my fault," I thought. "I deserve to feel this way."

I didn't have the energy to clean my own home. Washing the dishes was a major accomplishment. For someone who tends to be compulsively neat, not having the ambition or ability to get down on my knees to clean the corners was like saying goodbye to a part of myself. It was a death of sorts. Fortunately, my work as a writer allowed me to continue to support myself from home, but not without much pushing and self-directed pep talks.

But the most insidious and pernicious effect of my condition was that it robbed me of the simple pleasures in life. It left me too tired to see friends and family. I was losing them, yet I was powerless to stop this impending train wreck.

God, I firmly believe, led me to interview Shirley Williams and her mentor, Dr. William Stimack. Dr. Stimack opened up a whole new world to me. Through detox and a healthy way of eating, my life has changed dramatically.

I've been able to decrease my use of allopathic medicines, with the intention of one day being chemical-free. And as I alter my habits, I lose weight steadily and safely, and have never felt deprived or hungry. When I get an urge for something worthy of a four-star restaurant, I experiment and tweak recipes to make them good-for-you gourmet. Who says you can't have your tofu cake and eat it, too?

The biggest benefit, however, has come in the form of energy. I still have my flare-up days, but they are short-lived. Now I have the energy to work and live and love again.

If ever there was a poster girl for Dr. Stimack's program, it is I. My association with him as a patient and a colleague has proved to be one of the best experiences of my life.

The detox program, under the guidance of a qualified naturopath, just might be one of the best things you can do for yourself, too.

Barbara Rolek

CHAPTER ONE

OUR FOOD IS KILLING US

Healthcare trends come and go. But along the way some truths have emerged, the most important of which is the notion that food plays a significant role in our health.

It's time we really start looking closely at what we're eating, and why is it important for us to do that? Because our food is killing us.

A perfect example of that can be found in a study conducted by Dr. Fred Grey in 1946 for the United States government. He analyzed a bowl of spinach for its nutritional content. It was noted and filed away. He made the same test in 1962, and found that it took 12 bowls of spinach to equal the one bowl he tested in 1946. Prior to retiring, he did one final test in 1992 for the government, and found that it took 78 bowls of spinach to equal the same nutritional value of one bowl of 1946 spinach.[1] That's pretty overwhelming.

Another example is the story of Ray Grimes of Body Wise International, the maker of nutritional and skin care products, who bought one of the largest tomato farms in California in about 1978. Prior to assuming ownership, he had the tomatoes analyzed for their nutritional content. He was satisfied with what he saw, but thought he could make them even better, so he bought the 10,000-acre farm.

In the years that he owned it, he was able to produce a much heartier tomato with less blemishes that were much deeper red

---

[1]Dr. Patrick Quillen, *Beating Cancer with Nutrition* (Nutrition Times Press).

in color. When he decided to sell the farm, he had the tomatoes analyzed so he could show off to a potential buyer.

The analysis revealed that his tomatoes had no nutritional value. He had done so much tinkering with the soil by injecting it with pesticides, herbicides and other chemicals, all the tomatoes were good for was fiber and looking at.

Grimes went back to normal farming procedures. But it took him almost four years to turn the soil around and produce tomatoes with enough nutritional content so he could sell the farm.[2]

Bigger, faster, cheaper is never better and that's what we, as a society, have come to expect.

Now irradiating food is the latest "improvement." Irradiating food means microwaving it to kill bacteria so it has a longer shelf life. But the microwaves kill both good *and* bad bacteria and destroy the nutritional content.

We don't want irradiated food, we want organic food. Organic farming is a system of agriculture that uses environmentally sound techniques for raising crops and livestock that are free from most synthetic pesticides, growth hormones, and antibiotics. Organic farmers typically rely on pesticides and fertilizers derived from plants, animal wastes, and minerals. They incorporate biological methods, such as the use of one organism to suppress another, to help control pests. The methods used in organic farming increase soil fertility, balance insect populations, and reduce air, soil and water pollution.

But the rules for organic farmers aren't fair. Consider this: On the one hand, you have a small farmer who has had organic soil for the past 30 years and has produced good-quality foods.

_____

[2]From a conversation with Mr. Grimes in 1990.

On the other hand, a farmer who has injected ammonia, herbicides and pesticides into his soil, can call himself organic after just one year of stopping the use of chemicals. That came about because the large farms lobbied to have the definition of "organic food" changed so they could get in on the organic boom.

We're genetically modifying or bioengineering everything now. Randall Niedz, a researcher with the United States Horticultural Research Laboratory in Fort Pierce, Fla., estimates that in the United States the percentage of genetically engineered crops is now 60 to 80 percent.[3]

A farmer can no longer use the seed off his corn to plant next year's crop because it won't grow; he has to buy new seeds every year. We're changing the molecular structure of the corn under the pretext of making a better ear of corn.

Peter Cleary, a spokesman for the Grocery Manufacturers of America, estimates that 60 to 70 percent of the food on grocery store shelves may contain genetically modified food,[4] or as Europeans call it, "Frankenfood." The biggest concern is that a gene from a product that many people are allergic to can end up unexpectedly in a food without appearing on the label. That's frightening and it can be life-threatening.

New types of antibiotics are constantly being formulated because we are bombarded with so many of them in our foods, we are becoming antibiotic-resistant.

It is a proven fact that DDT causes cancer and is illegal for United States farmers to use, yet we still manufacture it and sell

---

[3]J. T. Harris, "It's in the Genes," *Post-Tribune*, September 5, 2001, p. D1.
[4]*Ibid.*

3

it to Third-World countries who use it on the produce they sell back to us.

Money drives everything. The government will sell us out and lead us down a primrose path for the almighty buck.

The only thing that's changed from 2,000 years ago is it takes more than 30 pieces of silver to sell us out. But not much more.

Look at the Food and Drug Administration, which has the most intelligent scientists, farmers and biologists who truly understand the problem but are unable to fix it because it's political. It's the lobby that will control what the FDA is able to do.

We, the public, are being duped by everyone.

We need to be in control of what we eat. The public should be making health decisions, not the government, the chicken factories and the veal barns. We have to take a stand and demand food the way God intended us to have it—natural and organic. As Albert Finney's character did in the movie *Network,* we have to throw open our collective windows and shout out, "I'm mad as hell and I'm not going to take it anymore."

If you believe in me and I believe in you and we believe in God, how can good health be denied us? We have a God-given right to be healthy without chemicals.

With the facts at hand, I can truly say, tell me how long you want to live, and I'll tell you what to eat to get there.

CHAPTER TWO

FOOD AS MEDICINE

Let food be your medicine and medicine be your food.

—Hippocrates

Can food truly be a medicine? The answer is absolutely, positively, resoundingly, yes. If you look at the allopathic (prescription) medicine of today, 50 percent is derived from edible plants.

UCLA conducted a study which showed that using food as a drug had always been important until the modern drug industry arose in the Twentieth Century. Prior to World War II, many herbs were listed side by side with chemical drugs in the United States pharmacopoeia of accepted medicine. Over 50 percent of the prescribed drugs come from Rain Forest botanicals and another almost 20 percent are chemical imitations of a plant, such as dandelion.

Dandelion is still used in salads, made into wine and cooked with other greens. It has a stimulating effect on the circulation, is a mild diuretic and a roasted version of dandelion is used for edema with great success. It's used primarily in patients who have severe allergies to allopathic water pills.

The pharmaceutical companies created the drugs so they could monopolize the market. They manufactured the medicines by isolating the active ingredient in a plant and replicating it synthetically. They took away the plant sources from the doctors, touting chemicals as being more reliable and easier to dose. The truth of the matter is herbal medications, which are essentially food, couldn't be patented because food can't be patented. And if you don't have a patent, you don't make money.

Another example is white willow bark. It has been used for thousands of years for headache and neuralgia-type pain. Pharmaceutical companies isolated the ingredient, synthesized it and it's now the active ingredient in aspirin, and it has been a real money-maker for them. But for people allergic to aspirin, taking white willow bark in its pure form would not be toxic to them. It's all the fillers the companies add to medications that are toxic to people.

CHAPTER THREE

THE BODY IS A CONVERTER

Why is food killing us? Our body is a converter, strictly a converter. It converts water, air, sunshine and food into living tissue and energy, and eliminates the waste. If we don't give it good-quality air, water, food and sunshine, it's just like a car that isn't properly maintained.

Low-grade fuel, such as fast-food, beef, pork, chicken, refined sugar, iodine, salt, and white flour, makes our engines start to miss, our cylinders get clogged up, and soon our mechanic is telling us we need a major overhaul. We have high blood pressure, high cholesterol, blocked arteries, heart failure, diabetes, kidney failure, chronic obstructive pulmonary disease (COPD), congestive heart failure, migraines, autoimmune diseases, to name a few.

The number one cause of intestinal cancer is eating meat. The number one cause of stomach cancer is stress, and the number one cause of liver or spleen cancer is the air we breathe.[5]

Can all these things be corrected by eating properly? Absolutely.

The renowned Dr. Dean Ornish has proved what a good diet can do for the heart. Many of Dr. Ornish's patients who were sent home to die by other medical professionals are now living a healthy life by simply changing their eating habits and being on a good exercise program.

---

[5]National Institutes of Health Conference on Alternative Therapies for Cancer, 2000.

The food of forty or fifty years ago didn't have carcinogens in it, nor did the air or water. But now, that's what has happened. We've killed the air, the water and the food.

In the water we drink, nationwide, over 2,100 organic and inorganic chemicals have been identified. Of that number, 156 are pure carcinogens. Of those, 26 are tumor promoters, which means if you have a tumor, they make them larger.

But, of course, that information, from tests conducted by the Environmental Protection Agency, has never been disseminated to the public by that agency, it came from a Ralph Nader organization in Washington, D.C.

CHAPTER FOUR

WHAT'S THE FIRST STEP?

The first step in using food as medicine is a course of detoxification or cleansing. For eight to fifteen weeks, no beef, pork, poultry, dairy, white sugar, chocolate, caffeine, white flour, or non-iodized salt are to be eaten while the body is purged of harmful toxins.

Drinking and cooking with steam-distilled water, eating soy products, cold-water fish and shellfish, fresh fruits and lightly steamed vegetables, and getting exercise are also part of the program.

Taking a special combination of herbs, such as dandelion, milk thistle, yarrow, and other supplements in capsule form facilitate the removal of undigested food, fecal matter, the remains of dead microorganisms and other waste products from the intestine, blood, cells and organs.

There are only eight things that can go wrong with our bodies—immune dysfunction, faulty metabolism, stress, environmental toxicity, pain and swelling (inflammation), liver and kidney dysfunction, female hormone dysfunction and faulty digestion.

The purpose of detoxification is to clean out the bowel, bladder, kidney, liver, lungs, blood and brain. After the organs are cleansed, the proper diet must be maintained so the organs won't become polluted again.

The liver does 950 life-saving functions and we plug it up with all these chemicals the body can't identify. No wonder we get sick! When the immune system is right, we *can't* get sick.

Here's how the GI tract works. It is composed of our mouth, esophagus, stomach, small intestine, large intestine, pancreas and liver. Each has a specific role and is extremely important.

The *mouth* is where digestion begins. Chewing stimulates the production of digestive enzymes in the stomach. The enzymes present in saliva start the breakdown of carbohydrates and fats. Food is then carried through the esophagus to the stomach.

In the *stomach*, hydrochloric acid and digestive enzymes continue the breakdown of protein, fat and carbohydrates. The partially digested food then moves to the small intestine.

The *small intestine* is where the bulk of digestion and absorption takes place. Various enzymes continue the breakdown of fats, carbohydrates and proteins. Bile, produced by the liver, is important for fat digestion and absorption.

As food travels through the 25 feet of small intestine, it is reduced to sugars, amino acids and fatty acids, which are then absorbed through the wall of the small intestine. The remaining unabsorbable matter accumulates forming the stool, which moves down to the large intestine.

The *large intestine,* or colon, continues the process of digestion by removing water from the waste matter. Water extraction compresses the fecal material and prepares it for elimination.

There are trillions of bacteria, yeasts and parasites living in our intestines, and the vast majority of these are helpful to our health. But a minority can cause disease. That's why maintaining the right balance is so vital to the well being of our bodies.

As we get older, there is a slow but definite decline in the level of digestive enzymes produced by the stomach, pancreas and small intestine. This leads to a decrease in digestion and absorption of nutrients and increased accumulation of rancid fecal matter in the intestinal tract.

Undigested food material and waste can also build up due to sluggish elimination, setting the stage for various health problems. In this toxic environment, beneficial bacteria die and are replaced by pathogenic, or disease-causing, organisms, such as parasites and yeasts. This leads to changes in the intestinal wall, allowing absorption of many toxic chemicals into the bloodstream.

As a result, the toxic load of the body increases and places additional burdens on the liver and kidneys, our main organs of detoxification and elimination. In short, instead of being a functional system that supplies the nutrients we need and eliminates the waste that we don't, our GI tract turns into a gigantic waste dump.

This is a problem that is made worse by the use of alcohol, junk food, prescription and over-the-counter medications, antibiotics, painkillers and diets high in fat and sugar while being low in fiber.

The first symptoms of an impaired digestive system are belching, bloating, gas, indigestion and constipation. Others may include decreased energy, headaches, fatigue and reduced resistance to infections.

As the GI tract continues to deteriorate, more serious problems can appear—everything from asthma, allergies and arthritis to cancer. Many autoimmune diseases, such as rheumatoid arthritis, scleroderma, and lupus have been linked to poor digestive function. Chronic skin conditions, such as psoriasis, eczema and hives, have also been linked.

In short, faulty digestion and bacterial imbalance can be traced to most chronic conditions known today. Why? It's pretty clear. Every organ and tissue of the body depends on the intestine for their nutrients; if the intestine is toxic and dysfunctional, then the blood and all the organs will be toxic as well.

Even if we eat a balanced diet, exercise, take nutritional supplements and otherwise take care of our health, our GI tracts still need help. That's because the declining production of enzymes, increasing numbers of bad bacteria and accumulation of waste within our intestines affects everyone. Plus the older we are, the worse the condition is.

Every time we eat sweets, any kind of junk food, drink coffee or alcohol or use antibiotics, painkillers, antacids, etc., our stomach and intestines become a little more dysfunctional.

The digestive system is like the roots of a tree. When the roots are strong, the tree is strong and healthy. When the roots are diseased, the whole tree suffers. That's why normal digestion, good absorption, and proper bacterial balance all play crucial roles in the health of the whole body.

And that's why detox is so important, possibly the most important thing you'll ever do.

CHAPTER FIVE

WHAT NOT TO EAT

What changes should you make immediately to eat your way to better health?

Avoid the five whites: iodized salt, refined white sugar, processed white flour, dairy products, and white fat which includes beef, veal, pork, chicken, lamb, and goat.

We don't have to eat meat in order to be healthy. There are much better sources of protein and calcium out there despite the commercials put out by the meat and dairy industries.

We want to avoid salt because it causes fluid retention and builds up at the cellular level. When we have too much sodium in our system, it blocks the cells from getting the proper nutrients and plays havoc with our blood pressure by overwhelming the sodium-potassium pump.

The daily recommended allowance of sodium is less than 2,400 mg. One teaspoon of salt contains 2,300 mg. of sodium. A couple of slices of pizza and you've exceeded your sodium allowance for the day!

Sugar, in addition to having a substantial calorie load, increases glucose levels which is a problem for both diabetics and those with low blood-sugar. It also feeds infections, such as yeast infections, and affects the eyes.

And don't think the answer is to be found in Aspartame, either.

Aspartame is the technical name for the brand names, NutraSweet, Equal, Spoonful, and Equal-Measure. Aspartame was discovered by accident in 1965, when James Schlatter, a chemist of G.D. Searle Company was testing an anti-ulcer drug. Aspartame was approved for dry goods in 1981 and for carbonated beverages in 1983.

Aspartame is, by far, one of the most dangerous food additives on the market today, accounting for over 75 percent of the adverse food reactions reported to the United States Food and Drug Administration.[6]

A few of the 90 different documented symptoms were headaches, dizziness, seizures, nausea, numbness, muscle spasms, weight gain, rashes, depression, fatigue, irritability, insomnia, vision problems, hearing loss, heart palpitations, breathing difficulties, anxiety attacks, slurred speech, loss of taste, memory loss and joint pain.

According to researchers and physicians studying the adverse effects of Aspartame, the following chronic illnesses are said to be triggered or worsened by Aspartame: Brain tumors, hormonal problems, multiple sclerosis, ALS, epilepsy, chronic fatigue syndrome, Parkinson's disease, Alzheimer's, lymphoma, fibromyalgia, and diabetes.

Why doesn't the public hear about these things? The reason is probably twofold. The first is lack of awareness by the general population. Aspartame-caused diseases are not reported in the newspapers like plane crashes. This is because these incidents occur one at a time in thousands of different locations across the United States.

The second is that most people do not associate their symptoms with the long-term use of Aspartame.

How Aspartame was approved is a lesson in how chemical and pharmaceutical companies can manipulate government

---

[6]Gold, Mark D., *Blazing Tattles,* Vol. 4, Nos. 4, 5, 6, April-June 1995.

agencies such as the FDA, "bribe" organizations such as the American Dietetic Association, and flood the scientific community with flawed and erroneous studies funded by the makers of Aspartame.[7]

Some of the more unusual places where Aspartame can be found is in laxatives, multivitamins, pharmaceuticals, and wine coolers. Know your product; read the labels!

White flour, unless it's organic, is dead. The milling process involves such a heat buildup, all the nutrients are killed. There's nothing left alive or healthy in it. They are just empty calories.

As far as milk goes, they didn't have to add vitamin D to it years ago. It was already there. They didn't take anything out and they didn't put anything in. Milk that goes straight from cow to bottle after being filtered is called raw milk, a milk Americans knew right up until World War II.

When an animal feeds on dried hay, its milk is slightly golden, exceptionally rich and almost sweet. When left to stand, a full head of cream rises to the top of the bottle. And when it sours, or clabbers, perfectly healthful dishes can be made with it.

Old-time farmers will tell you they can tell where their cows have been grazing by the taste of the milk. Put an animal on grass instead of dried hay, and the milk will change, becoming less creamy and more flowery tasting.

Supermarket milk will be uniformly white, its cream won't rise and a lactic perfume will be detectable only if the milk is boiled.

This milk, from hormone-injected cows, is standardized, fortified, pasteurized and homogenized. It is taken apart and

---

[7]*Ibid.*

15

put back together again, not always in the same proportions. Then it is cooked and emulsified. Is it still milk? It's the milk we know. It should really be called a "reconstituted milk-flavored beverage"[8]—all in the name of pooling vast quantities of milk, prolonging shelf life and the notion that drinking raw milk is risky.

Today, selling raw milk is illegal in most states and, where it is allowed, the bottle carries the warning that it "may contain disease-causing microorganisms." How risky is raw milk? Probably as risky as drinking milk from hormone-injected cows.

And why shouldn't we eat meat? We know that steroids and growth hormones are being injected into cattle and into the feed in poultry.

Those steroids work the same way on animals as they do on football players and wrestlers. It's almost certain that athletes who inject steroids will develop some sort of cancer or tumors. If we're so certain that this will happen to humans, why wouldn't it happen to a cow?

If you were to go on a tour of a slaughterhouse, you'd probably never eat meat again. Cows are covered with tumors which are merely circled with purple ink, cut out, and the remainder of the meat is put on the market. Surely there are cancer cells in the animal's blood, and, therefore, in every ounce of its meat, tumor-free or not.

The number one polluter in the world is the cow. Its feces give off methane gas which pollutes the air, and its urine pollutes the ground water.

---

[8]Emily Green, "Is Milk Still Milk?", *Los Angeles Times*, August 2, 2000.

The amount of grain and clean water it takes to feed one cow could be used to feed hundreds of people. It doesn't make sense to feed cows. Let's eliminate the middle man.

And even if the meat is free of hormones and steroids, the overwhelming truth is that white fat turns into cholesterol, goes right to our arteries and winds up as plaque. In addition, meat remains in the digestive system a minimum of 24 hours and for as long as five years. It gets caught in the diverticuli, gets rancid, and gives off toxic gases that are absorbed by the system making us feel sluggish, tired, and rundown.

We're the only long-intestined animal to eat meat, yet we don't have the teeth to eat meat. Elephants don't eat meat and they've managed to make it pretty darn well without it. A gorilla is a vegetarian and it is one of the strongest animals known to man.

It's not always entirely possible to do this, but when a fresh alternative is available, avoid eating food products in cans because the chemicals used to coat the cans so they don't rust can leach into our foods.

Avoid drinking coffee, especially decaffeinated coffee which contains adverse chemicals used in the processing, because it sucks the water right out of our systems. For every cup of coffee we drink, it is necessary to drink two and a half cups of water to balance things out. Coffee is also known to trigger arthritis pain.

What else should we avoid? Antiperspirants. Deodorant is fine, but antiperspirants contain aluminum chlorhydrate. Every Alzheimer's patient who has been tested shows high levels of aluminum in his body. Is there a link? Probably.

The same is true of cooking in aluminum pots. Use stainless steel instead and avoid using aluminum foil and baking powder containing aluminum.

17

CHAPTER SIX

WHAT YOU SHOULD EAT

What should you eat and eat in moderation?

Cold-water fish, fresh fruit, fresh vegetables, whole grains, nuts, and beans. Salads with dark, leafy greens such as spinach and march grass. Short-grain brown rice and soy products such as soy milk, tofu, tempeh, miso, soy burgers, soynut butter, and soy-based "meats," which are better sources of calcium and protein than meat and dairy.

Brown rice is basically unpolished whole grain rice with the bran left intact; only the inedible hull has been removed, making it highly nutritious. Milling is the primary difference between brown and white rice. The benefits of brown rice are its immunity-enhancing properties, it helps lower cholesterol, it's an effective laxative and yields high dietary fiber.

Brown rice is low in fat, cholesterol-free, gluten-free, salt-free, high in vitamins B and E, is filling and is a perfect grain for diabetics as the fiber content and complex carbohydrates keep the blood sugars in check.

There are several alternatives to refined white sugar—raw turbinado sugar, beet sugar, sucanat (organic natural cane sugar), date sugar, fructose, barley malt, rice syrup, corn syrup, molasses, maple syrup and local raw honey, which can have dramatic, positive effects for those suffering with allergies, sinus and other conditions.

Bee pollen is one of the oldest and safest natural remedies known to man. Honeybee pollen is a highly concentrated source of vitamins, minerals, enzymes, lecithin, hormone-like substances and a natural anti-bacterial substance in a base of protein, carbohydrates and fatty acids.

Pollen has been reported to benefit the endocrine glands, prevent anemia, strengthen the immune system, improve bowel function, help protect the heart arteries from atherosclerosis, treat prostate conditions, benefit brain and nerves, clear up some cases of acne, counteract fatigue, increase longevity and more.

One can't talk about sweeteners without mentioning stevia. This subtropical herb native to Paraguay and parts of Brazil is 300 times sweeter than cane sugar. One-half teaspoon of powdered white stevia contains less than one calorie and less than one-half gram of carbohydrates. It doesn't raise blood-sugar levels and prevents tooth decay!

In 1991, the FDA banned the importation of stevia. The leaf powder of which has been used for hundreds of years as an alternative sweetener. It is used widely in Japan with no adverse effects. Scientists involved in reviewing stevia have declared it to be safe for human consumption—something which has been well known in many parts of the world where it is not banned. Many people believe stevia was banned to keep the product from taking hold in the U.S. and cutting into sales of Aspartame.

For years, it has been kept on the shelves of health food stores and sold as a dietary supplement because the FDA considers it an unapproved food additive and will not allow it to be sold as a sweetener. That's why you won't find it on the shelf next to the Aspartame. But since the Dietary Supplement Act of 1994 allows stevia to be sold as a supplement in health food stores, the word is getting out.

Now, especially in California, you can find pots of stevia being sold alongside kitchen herbs like rosemary and basil. And online seed catalogs are offering stevia seeds.[9]

Many people take a leaf, crush it to release the oil and put it in their tea or oatmeal, but there is also processed stevia, in green or white powders, and liquid extract. Fresh-leaf stevia tastes the best; it's mild and refreshing with a slight licorice aftertaste. Just be careful; processed stevia is so concentrated, a little goes a long way.

In 1999, the FDA ruled that soy, along with a low-fat, low-cholesterol diet, can reduce the risk of coronary heart disease, but that's just one of the benefits of soy.

Soy products contain anticarcinogenic compounds and, therefore, are effective cancer preventatives. Soy increases bone density, and because it contains thiamin (vitamin B1), it balances the emotions by clearing the mind and stabilizing mood. Soy reduces the risk of colon polyps, and, because of its estrogen-like effects, offers relief from menopausal symptoms by easing hot flashes. And because soy has naturally occurring isoflavones which act as antioxidants (which are known to quench free radicals), it may lessen the overall likelihood of cancer.

You can get your share of soy in various products—milk, tofu, veggie burgers and on and on.

Eat lots of fruits (be careful if you're a diabetic) and lightly steamed vegetables. Organics are best, but that's not always available or economically feasible. In either case, always wash your produce well with steam-distilled water.

---

[9]Drake, Laurie, "Stevia: So Sweet, Natural and So L.A.," *Chicago Tribune*, June 6, 2001.

Whole wheat flours and rice flours are much better choices than white flour. When a product contains whole grains, such as oats, whole wheat, and rye, all of the grain, except for the nonedible husk, is used. In comparison, white flour is refined, which means that the other parts of the wheat kernel (the bran and germ) are removed.

The problem with this is when you remove these parts, you also remove nutrients such as iron, zinc, fiber, and some B vitamins. Because of these nutrient losses, white bread must be fortified with the B vitamins—thiamin, riboflavin, niacin, folate—and iron.

Additionally, other nutrients are lost in this refining process and not replaced. For example, enriched white bread has only 24 percent of the fiber, 36 percent of the zinc, 18 percent of the vitamin B6, and 23 percent of the magnesium found in whole-grain bread.

Be careful when buying bread, however. The words "100 percent whole wheat" should be smack on the label, and "whole wheat flour" should be the only type of flour used for a loaf of bread to legitimately call itself whole wheat. Whole grain breads can use other grains such as oats, rye, buckwheat, and potatoes, but the bread may not be made with 100 percent whole grains. Read the ingredient listings to make sure whole grain flour is used predominantly. Natural Ovens out of Manitowoc, Wisc., puts out a wonderful line of natural bread products.

What can you drink? Organic milk is one option. It undergoes conventional processing but is certified to have come from hormone- and antibiotic-free cows which have been raised on feed produced without the use of chemical fertilizers, pesticides and herbicides. Another option is BST-free milk.

This signifies that cattle are not treated with the genetically engineered milk-boosting hormone bovine somatotropin.

Raw milk is a good choice, but unless it's certified or you know the farmer producing it, what he feeds his cows and if he injects them, drink certified organic soy milk or rice milk instead.

Let's take a look at soy milk. It's lactose free and comes in regular, flavored and low-fat varieties. An eight-ounce glass of regular soy milk serves up about four grams of fat and is low in saturated fat, with only half a gram per serving. Reduced-fat soy milk has only two grams of fat per cup. Because it's made from plant-based soybeans, soy milk is cholesterol free and has three grams of fiber.

When it comes to water, drink only steam-distilled water because that is the only filtering process which removes all the harmful toxins. You can drink water with your meals, but the body won't recognize it as water and will see it as food. Drink water between meals and 8 to 10 glasses a day.

Another good beverage is any Chinese organic tea. They are low in caffeine and have a positive effect on the system because they are natural, leafy and good for you.

Eat only cold-water fish, such as cod, tuna, halibut, salmon, scrod, herring, and tilapia. Warm-water fish are polluted and contain high levels of mercury. Farm-raised fish are no better because they are predominantly genetically modified to increase their size.

After hundreds of studies, the FDA recently approved a heart-healthy claim that Omega-3 fatty acids, found in fish such as salmon, lead to a decrease in fatty deposits in the blood and an increase in HDL (good) cholesterol.[10]

What is considered a safe fat? Any oil that gets hard at room temperature is a killer. The best oils to use are canola, sunflower, safflower, olive, peanut, sesame, and soybean, and a few others. Make sure to buy them in small quantities so they don't get rancid. Don't use nonstick cooking sprays because they contain harmful chemicals.

Eat lubricating fat. Alphalinolenic acid, a heart-healthy fat found in some foods, also has anti-inflammatory properties. Foods rich in alphalinolenic acid include vegetables, beans, fruits, flaxseed oil, wheat germ and canola oil.

Eat ginger every day. Gingerroot also has anti-inflammatory properties. It works like ibuprofen, but without the side effects. But you have to eat it every day to feel the results. You don't have to use a lot; slice it into stir-fry vegetables, or mix it with boiling water to make a delicious tea (see recipes).

Use sea salt instead of table salt. Sea salt, a whole salt, contains a wide variety of minerals and trace elements and is a vitally important part of our diet. Common table salt lacks these minerals and trace elements because it is purified and refined, leaving only sodium and chloride. After refining, common table salt is mixed with iodine, bleaching agents, and anti-caking agents to create a purely white, free-flowing product.

Iodine is a natural element required by the human body for proper physical and mental development (to prevent goiters and retardation among other things). Most people receive sufficient amounts of iodine from the daily diets, but more than one

---

[10]Anthony Almada, "A Real Fish Story," *Delicious Living*, April 2001.

billion people in other countries are at risk of iodine deficiency because their soil lacks it and they lack access to foods which contain iodine.

The disadvantage to iodized salt is that calcium and magnesium get eliminated and aluminum and sugar are added as stabilizing elements. Those are irritants to the thyroid and can create imbalances and the body can develop difficulties metabolizing refined salt.

CHAPTER SEVEN

A WORD ABOUT WATER

Good nutrition is the most important principal of good health. When talking about good nutrition, you can't ignore good water. What should we be drinking? Steam-distilled water only. Even in our local area, there are water supplies that are so contaminated, they're very close to being banned as drinking water.

Ask yourself, are you drinking all the water you should every day? We've all heard the medical experts recommend at least eight glasses a day. And we've all been thirsty. Here are a few facts to help you consider whether you ought to visit the well a little more frequently than you are.

Seventy-five percent of Americans are chronically dehydrated. In 37 percent of Americans, the thirst mechanism is so weak that it is often mistaken for hunger. Even mild dehydration will slow down one's metabolism as much as three percent. One glass of water shut down midnight hunger pangs for almost 100 percent of the dieters in a 1977 University of Washington study.

A lack of water is the number one trigger of daytime fatigue. And research indicates that 8 to 10 glasses of water a day can significantly ease back and joint pain for up to 80 percent of sufferers.

A mere two percent drop in body water can trigger fuzzy short-term memory, trouble with basic math and difficulty focusing on a computer screen or a printed page.

Dr. William D. Stimack and Barbara Rolek

Drinking five glasses of clean water daily decreases the risk of colon cancer by 45 percent, can slash the risk of breast cancer by 79 percent, and reduce the likelihood of developing bladder cancer by 50 percent.

CHAPTER EIGHT

NEXT TIME

The Chinese feel the balance of energy in the body is true health. Too many people think health is the absence of disease. Health is not the absence of disease. Health is loving life to the fullest, feeling life to the fullest, and sharing life to the fullest.

It's time to wrap up this book which started as a way to provide patients with recipes to assist them in following the detox plan and diet. It has evolved into much more than that, but there's still so much more to talk about.

In our second book, we will explore why detox is essential to life.

We hope you will join us in continuing to seek health and happiness. In the meantime, promise yourself:

To be so strong that nothing can disturb your peace of mind.

To talk health, happiness and prosperity to every person you meet.

To make all your friends feel that there is something in them.

To look at the sunny side of everything and make your optimism come true.

To think only of the best, to work only for the best and to expect only the best.

Dr. William D. Stimack and Barbara Rolek

To be just as enthusiastic about the success of others as you are about your own.

To forget the mistakes of the past and press on to the greater achievements of the future.

To wear a cheerful countenance at all times and give every living creature you meet a smile.

To give so much time to the improvement of yourself that you have no time to criticize others.

To be too large for worry, too noble for anger, too strong for fear, and too happy to permit the presence of trouble.

"The Optimist's Creed" by Christian D. Larson

CHAPTER NINE

BEFORE YOU START COOKING

So you've decided to take charge of your life. You're on detox. Now what? What can there possibly be for you to eat? Plenty! No bread-and-water diet for you (unless it's whole wheat and steam distilled). There's more, so much more.

We know how to eat right. You've heard it all before.

We should eat a variety of foods, including 6 to 11 servings of grains a day, 3 to 5 servings of vegetables, 2 to 4 servings of fruits, 2 to 3 servings of dairy or dairy substitutes, and 2 to 3 servings of protein.

We know that we should limit our total fat to 30 percent of our daily calories. So if we're on a 2,000-calorie diet, we should consume no more than 67 grams of fat a day.

We know to limit our saturated fat to no more than 10 percent of our daily calories and not to consume more than 300 mg. of cholesterol daily.

On the simplest level, then, this means eating whole-wheat bread, soy cheese, fresh fruit, a whole-wheat tortilla with lightly steamed or roasted vegetables, broiled fish, green leafy salads. And when you get tired of that, these recipes should keep your interest level high.

Before we start cooking, here are a few words about labels.

Understanding the Nutrition Facts Food Label

There's nothing mysterious about the nutrition facts food label. It can be found on most packaged products in the grocery store. Its purpose is to list nutrients considered to be important to today's health-conscious consumer. They are total fat, saturated fat, cholesterol, sodium, carbohydrates and fiber.

The Percent of Daily Value is based on a 2,000-calorie diet and tells you if the food is high or low in a particular nutrient. It also shows how that food stacks up in an entire day's diet. As a rule of thumb, if the Daily Value is 5 % or less, the food contains only a small amount of that nutrient. Total fat, saturated fat, cholesterol and sodium with low Percent of Daily Value are good choices.

The Ingredients List is located in a separate location on the label. Ingredients are listed in descending order by weight; thus, if the first ingredient is sugar, there is more sugar in that product than anything else.

Example of a Nutrition Facts Food Label

Nutrition Facts
Serving Size 1 cup (228g)
Servings Per Container 2

Amount Per Serving

Calories 260   Calories from Fat 120

	% Daily Value*
Total Fat 13g	**20%**
Saturated Fat 5g	**25%**
Cholesterol 30mg	**10%**
Sodium 660mg	**28%**
Total Carbohydrate 31g	**10%**
Dietary Fiber 0g	**0%**
Sugars 5g	
Protein 5g	

Vitamin A 4%	•	Vitamin C 2%
Calcium 15%	•	Iron 4%

* Percent Daily Values are based on a 2,000 calorie diet. Your daily values may be higher or lower depending on your calorie needs:

	Calories:	2,000	2,500
Total Fat	Less than	65g	60g
Sat Fat	Less than	20g	25g
Cholesterol	Less than	300mg	300mg
Sodium	Less than	2,400mg	2,400mg
Total Carbohydrate		300g	375g
Dietary Fiber		25g	30g

Calories per gram:
Fat 9 • Carbohydrate 4 • Protein 4

Recommended Dietary Allowances*

The following Recommended Dietary Allowances (RDAs) are based on a 2,000-calorie diet. Your daily values may be higher or lower depending on your calorie needs.

Total Fat	Less than	65 g
Saturated Fat	Less than	20 g
Cholesterol	Less than	300 mg
Sodium	Less than	2,400 mg
Total Carbohydrate		300 g
Dietary Fiber		25 g
Protein		50 g
Calcium		800 mg
Iron		15 mg

Calories per gram: Fat = 9; Carbohydrate = 4; Protein = 4

Light, Low Fat and Cholesterol Free

What do these words really mean? Some food packages make claims such as "light," "low fat," and "cholesterol free." These claims can only be used if a food meets strict government guidelines. Here are some of the meanings.

Calorie Free	Less than 5 calories
Low Calorie	40 calories or less
Light or Lite	1/3 fewer calories or 50% less fat
Light in Sodium	50% less sodium
Fat Free	3 g or less fat
Cholesterol Free	Less than 2 mg cholesterol and 2 g or less saturated fat

Low Cholesterol	20 mg or less cholesterol and 2 g or less saturated fat
Sodium Free	Less than 5 mg sodium
Very Low Sodium	35 mg or less sodium
Low Sodium	140 mg or less sodium
High Fiber	5 g or more fiber

A Word about Fats

Dietary fat can be divided into three different types: saturated, polyunsaturated, and monounsaturated.

Saturated Fats are generally solid at room temperature. They have been shown to increase blood cholesterol levels. Saturated fats are primarily found in animal products such as meat, butter, milk, cream and lard. Some plant foods, such as palm oil, coconut oil, vegetable shortening, and some peanut butters also contain large amounts of saturated fats.

Polyunsaturated Fats tend to lower blood cholesterol levels when used in moderation. These fats are found in high concentrations in vegetable oils, and are usually liquid at room temperature, such as sunflower oil, corn oil, safflower, sesame, soybean and cottonseed oils.

Monounsaturated Fats have also been shown to decrease cholesterol levels in the blood when used in moderation. They can be liquid or solid at room temperature, and are usually derived from plant sources. Olive, peanut, and canola oils are high in monounsaturated fats.

Dietary Cholesterol comes from animal sources such as meat, poultry, fish and other seafood and dairy products. Egg yolks and organ meats contain high amounts of dietary cholesterol.

Hydrogenation is a chemical process in which hydrogen is added to unsaturated oils to make them firmer at room temperature. Hydrogenated fats such as shortening or margarine are more saturated than the oil from which they are made.

Calculating Percentage of Fat in Food

The best choices, then, are polyunsaturated and monounsaturated fats and foods with 30 percent or less of total calories from fat. But how do you determine the percentage of a food's total calories that comes from fat? Use the following formula.

First, you need to know the total calories and the grams of fat per serving. Since each gram of fat contains 9 calories, you multiply the grams of fat by 9 to get the total calories from fat. Then divide that number by the total calories. Multiply this number by 100 and you will have the percent of total calories from fat. For example:

$$\frac{5 \text{ grams of fat} \times 9}{500 \text{ calories}} \times 100 = 9\% \text{ of total calories from fat}$$

A Word about Flour

No matter how hard they try, some people just can't get used to the taste of whole-wheat flour. Before you give up entirely, try some of the other healthy flours, such as spelt or rice flour.

But if all your best efforts fail and you simply can't exist without white flour, make it organic.

King Arthur® Flour is just one of the companies which offers organic white. They make two types. Organic Select Artisan Flour, which is milled from 100 percent certified organic hard red wheat and modeled after the lower-protein and higher-ash flours that are common in Europe. It is used to produce artisan-style breads.

The other type is Organic Baker's Classic Flour, which is milled from 100 percent certified organic hard red spring wheat and is suitable for a range of bakery products.

A Word about Tofu

Tofu's not the prettiest kid on the block. But it's one of the most versatile proteins around. Because its flavor is so benign, it soaks up all the wonderful flavors surrounding it. Tofu can be diced, sliced, blended and creamed in so many foods. There are typically three different textures in your supermarket and each lends itself to a different culinary usage:

Firm Tofu: It has a solid texture, thus can be cut into cubes, slices, strips and is great in stews, soups, chili, tomato sauce, stir fries, salads or stuffed into pitas. Slice it length-wise and marinate it in salad dressing or barbecue sauce for meaty tofu steaks under the broiler. You can even mash it and combine it with bread crumbs, oats, and some spices for your own tofu burgers.

Soft Tofu: Combine soft tofu with salsa for a dip with a kick or whip it in the blender with fruit, ice, and soy milk for a quick fruit smoothie. Soft tofu can also be mixed with chives or green onions as a topping for potatoes or blended into soups.

Silken Tofu: Its creamy texture enables it to work as a replacement for the cream in creamy soups, salad dressings, and a chip dip. It's a dream in pumpkin pie and cheese cake. It can also be used as the base for vegetable spreads to smear on bagels, crackers, and in pitas.

There is also **baked tofu,** a precooked, ready-to-eat soy product which can be sliced and added to salads and sandwiches right from the package. It comes in several flavors and has a flavor reminiscent of smoked meats.

Substituting with Soy Products

Soy milk

- Substitute for cow's milk one-to-one in any recipe with good results
- Blend with frozen fruit and a wholesome sweetener, such as stevia, for a delicious dairy-free smoothie

Silken Tofu

- Blend into shakes, fruit smoothies, and puddings
- Substitute for sour cream in dips and dressings
- Replace eggs in baking: 1/4 cup = 1 egg

Soy Flour

- Replace up to 1/4 of the flour in quickbreads and pancakes
- Replace up to 1/8 of the flour in yeast bread recipes
- Use to thicken sauces and gravies
- Replace eggs in baking: 1 tablespoon soy flour + 1 tablespoon water = 1 egg[11]

How to Press Tofu

Tofu comes in a package that usually contains a lot of liquid. Always drain the liquid before using any variety of tofu. Usually, firm tofu is also pressed so that it can be cut and cooked without falling apart. Here's how to do it.

After draining off any excess water, sandwich firm tofu between two pieces of paper towels. Place this on a wire rack with a pan underneath to catch the drips. Next, place a cutting board, for example, on top of the tofu and weight it with a heavy object (a can of organic beans, for example!). Allow the tofu to drain for an hour or so. Remove weights and paper toweling and proceed with your recipe.

Another way to solidify tofu and enhance its ability to absorb seasonings and marinades is to cube it and boil in water for 10 minutes and then drain.

---

[11]Marie Oser, *More Soy Cooking*, p. 24.

MAKING BETTER CHOICES

<u>Food</u>	<u>Healthy Substitute</u>
Milk	Soy milk, rice milk (Silk, Eden Soy, Sun Soy)
Mayonnaise	Soy mayonnaise (Nayonaise)
Hamburgers	Veggie burgers (Boca Burger)
Cheeses	Soy cheeses (Veggie Shreds, Veggie Slices)
Butter	Veggie butter (made by Galaxy Foods)
Peanut Butter	SoyNut Butter and other nut butters
Salt	Non-iodized sea salt
White Sugar	Liquid stevia
Brown sugar	Sucanat
Salad Dressing	Lemon juice, orange juice, rice vinegar, Newman's Own
Eggs	Free-range organic eggs
Chocolate	Carob
White Flour	Whole-grain flour, spelt
Bread	Natural <u>whole</u> grain (NOT enriched or white flour)
Rice	Short-grain brown rice
Pasta	Whole-grain pasta
Ground Meat	Veggie ground (Gimme Lean)
Gravy Thickener	Arrowroot

IF I'M ON DETOX, CAN I OR CAN'T I?

<u>YES</u>	<u>NO</u>
Cold-water fish (fresh or frozen)	Chicken, beef, turkey, pork, lamb, etc.
Fresh and frozen vegetables	Canned foods
Fresh and frozen fruits (no added sugar)	Snacks: Candy, potato chips, etc.
Non-iodized salt (small amount)	Iodized salt
Short-grain brown rice	White rice
Stevia sweetener, honey (small amount)	Sugar (white and brown)
Veggie Slices (cheese alternative), soy milk	Dairy products
Whole-grain pasta, breads, pitas, bagels	White flour
Veggie burgers, soy, tofu, tempeh	Instant foods
Sweet potatoes	Anything that says "diet"
Potatoes (baked or boiled)	Anything with food color
Olive oil or cold-pressed canola oil	Anything saying "natural flavorings added"
Dressings (oil and vinegar or lemon juice)	Alcohol
Organic Eggs (1 or 2 weekly, if needed)	Wine
Steam-distilled water	Tap water

<u>YES</u>	<u>NO</u>
Herbal teas	Coffee, soft drinks, caffeine
V-8 Juice (no preservatives)	Decaffeinated coffee
Nuts, lentils and legumes	Preservatives and additives
Carob	Chocolate
Soynut butter and other nut butters	Peanut butter
Old-fashioned oatmeal (rolled oats)	Boxed cereals
Organic butter (cream and salt only)	Butter, margarine

GLOSSARY OF TERMS

Arrowroot: A starch extracted from the roots of certain plants growing in tropical countries, especially Florida and the West Indies. Arrowroot is more easily digested than other forms of starch. Like tapioca, flour or cornstarch, this powder can be used as a thickener.

Baking Powder: Use only low-sodium, aluminum-free, double-acting baking powder in cooking and baking.

Barley Malt: Substance obtained by allowing barley to soften in water and germinate. The enzyme diastase, developed during the germination process, catalyzes the hydrolysis of starch to the sugar maltose. Barley malt has a high protein and carbohydrate content. Available at health food and specialty stores.

Basmati Rice: A long-grain rice with a faintly nutlike flavor. Aromatic and available in a brown rice variety. Excellent flavor.

Brown Rice: Unpolished whole grain rice with the bran left on the endosperm after removal of the hull. Highly nutritious with short-grain brown rice being the best for you because it is the most unrefined. Available widely.

Brown Rice Syrup: A sweetener made from brown rice. For one cup brown rice syrup, substitute 3/4 cup plus 2 tablespoons pure maple syrup, or 1/2 cup molasses, or 3/4 cup barley malt syrup, or 3/4 cup plus 2 tablespoons honey.

Carob: Carob is a natural sweetener that comes from the pods of the carob tree. Inside the pods are tiny beans which are roasted and ground into carob powder, similar to cocoa. Carob is considered to be an excellent chocolate substitute and is high in minerals. Unlike chocolate, it is low in fat and has no caffeine.

Carob Chips: Similar to chocolate chips, sweetened carob chips are used in baking. Available at health food and specialty stores.

Carob Powder (Unsweetened): Similar to cocoa powder, carob powder comes in toasted and untoasted varieties (toasting helps bring out the flavor). Since carob burns more easily than cocoa, recipes using it call for lower temperatures. Available at health food and specialty stores.

Cold-Pressed Oil: Any oil that is obtained by pressing without heat, light or oxygen, thus extracting the oil without damaging the nutritional value or flavor of the final product.

Couscous: Tiny grains of pasta found in Middle Eastern cuisine. Sold in this country presteamed, couscous only needs to be added to boiling water or broth, stirred, removed from the heat, and set aside for 5 minutes to absorb the liquid. Available in plain, whole wheat, and other varieties.

Flaxseeds: The seeds of flax are tiny, smooth and flat, and range in color from a light gold to a reddish brown. They serve a variety of purposes, including oil production, baking and other food uses. A valuable source of Omega-3 fatty acids, flaxseed is produced and harvested in about the same manner as wheat and other small grains.

Flour: The finely ground sifted meal of any edible grain.

Kamut flour: Ground from a highly nutritious ancient wheat, kamut contains a unique type of gluten that is easier to digest than common wheat. Available in health food stores and specialty stores.

Oat flour: May be purchased from health food and specialty stores, or made at home by pulsing whole oats in a food processor. Oat flour contains some gluten and makes baked goods moister, chewier, and more crumbly.

Organic white flour: White wheat flour that is milled from 100 percent certified organic hard red wheat and modeled after the lower-protein and higher-ash flours that are common in Europe used to produce artisan-style breads, or milled from 100 percent certified organic hard red spring wheat and is suitable for a range of bakery products. Available widely and through King Arthur® Flour.

Rice flour: A flour made from the milling of a combination of white and brown rice that has little or no gluten.

Semolina flour: Made from coarsely ground durum wheat. Higher in protein with a firmer texture, makes excellent pastas.

Soy Flour: Finely ground flour made from soybeans which is very high in protein and low in carbohydrates. It is mixed with other flours because it contains no gluten. Soy flour is also used to bind sauces and replace eggs in baked goods. Available in health food stores and most supermarkets.

Spelt flour: Spelt is believed to be a relative of wheat, and it tastes like a mild version of it. Though it contains gluten, it is tolerated more easily by those with wheat allergies, and it's great for making pasta and bread. Spelt is high in protein, contains all eight of the essential amino acids, and is rich in Vitamin B. Available widely.

Whole-wheat flour: Whole-grain flour that contains the wheat germ. Whole-wheat flour, made from hard wheat, has the highest nutritional, fiber and fat content.

It must be refrigerated, because it contains the entire grain and can become rancid easily. Widely available.

Whole-wheat pastry flour: Finely milled whole-grain flour made from soft winter wheat is lower in gluten and excellent in cakes and quickbreads. Available in health food and specialty stores.

Gimme Lean: This is a meat alternative, made by Lightlife, available in sausage and ground beef styles and sold in the freezer section of health food stores and supermarkets.

Granulated Garlic: Garlic textured into grains, like sugar or salt. Far superior to garlic powder in flavor and aroma. Available at health food stores and some supermarkets.

Jasmine Rice: Fragrant rice similar to basmati rice which is popular in Thai cuisine. Available widely.

Lite Silken Tofu: A very low-fat tofu that is rich tasting and has a smooth, creamy texture and a custard-like consistency. Available widely.

Millet: A grain that is nutritious and gluten-free. It has a very mild flavor that can be improved by toasting the grains. Available at health food stores and in the health-food section of many supermarkets.

Mirin: Sweet Japanese rice wine used in cooking. Available widely.

Miso: Fermented soybean paste with the consistency of peanut butter. Miso should be stored in the refrigerator. It is excellent in soups, sauces, marinades, dips, salad dressings and main dishes. It comes in many varieties, including:

Barley miso: Reddish brown in color with a chunky, rich flavor.

Hatcho miso: Dark brown in color with overtones of chocolate. Unlike other miso which is fermented with grain, hatcho is made with soybeans only.

Mellow white miso: Pale beige in color with a mild, sweet fragrance. It is rich and creamy in texture and makes a great addition to sauces, fillings, dips and dressings.

Mochi: See Sweet Brown Rice.

Nayonaise: A tofu-based mayonnaise made by Nasoya. It has no eggs which means no cholesterol, and is lower in fat than traditional mayonnaise.

Oat Bran: A fiber-rich bran derived from oats that may be used in baked goods. Available widely.

Old-fashioned Rolled Oats: Another name for old-fashioned oatmeal. These are oat groats that are steamed, rolled and flaked so that they cook quickly. They are often cooked as a breakfast cereal, added raw to granola or muesli mixes, or used otherwise in cooking and baking.

Quinoa: Cultivated for centuries in South America, this grain is high in protein, calcium and iron and can be used like rice.

Recommended Dietary Allowances (RDAs): An RDA reflects the maximum allowable amount of a nutrient in the diet in order to maintain a healthy body.

Rice Milk: Non-dairy milk made from brown rice. Some varieties are gluten free, others are not. A common brand is Rice Dream. Always shake well before using because of settling. Rice milk is sweeter than soy milk and, thus, works well in most desserts but not in all savory dishes.

Sea Salt: Salt derived from evaporated seawater, which retains some natural minerals and contains no additives.

Seitan: This is a meat alternative made from wheat gluten. It is available packed in broth or shrink-wrapped and found in the refrigerated case at health food stores and some supermarkets.

Sesame Tahini: This is a paste made from ordinary white sesame seeds. It's used in the Middle East to make hummus, baba ghanouj, sauces and others dishes. The oil tends to rise to the top, so stir before using. To make your own, in a blender, mix white sesame seeds with a small amount of peanut oil until creamy. A substitute for tahini would be 3 parts soynut butter and 1 part sesame oil.

Silk: The Brand name used by White Wave products to describe its line of soy milk.

Soba Noodles: Buckwheat noodles that are high in fiber and protein and lower in fat than traditional pasta. Available at Asian markets and most supermarkets.

Soybeans:

> **Dried soybeans:** Sold in bulk in many health food stores and in one-pound packages from Arrowhead Mills. These must be presoaked for several hours before cooking.

> **Green soybeans (edamamé):** Green or immature soybeans used as a snack or appetizer. Available frozen at health food stores, Asian markets and some supermarkets.

> **Sweet beans:** Shelled green soybeans used in stir-fry dishes. They are sold frozen in one-pound packages in health food stores and some supermarkets.

Soy Burgers, Ground or Sausage: A ready-to-eat meat alternative found in the freezer section of health food stores and supermarkets under the Boca brand name and many others.

Soy Cream Cheese and Sour Cream: Vegan cream cheese and sour cream used in recipes calling for these two ingredients. Very close in texture and flavor to the original. Available widely.

Soy Milk: A nondairy beverage made by extracting the liquid from cooked soybeans. It is cholesterol-free and low in fat and sodium. It can be substituted one-to-one in recipes calling for cow's milk. Soy milk comes in 1%, vanilla and chocolate varieties. Widely available.

Soynut Butter: A peanut butter substitute made with soynuts that is much lower in saturated fat, sugar and cholesterol. Widely available.

Soynuts: Dried soybeans that have been roasted. They are similar to nuts and can be used as a snack or in salads. Available in most supermarkets.

Soyrizo Vegetarian Chorizo: This is a soy substitute for the highly seasoned Mexican pork sausage. Remove the casing and crumble before browning in a small amount of olive oil.

Stevia: An herb native to Paraguay and parts of Brazil which is 300 times sweeter than cane sugar. It comes powdered, as an extract, fresh and dried.

Sugars

Date sugar: Dehydrated date pieces that have been ground into a fine sugar. Date sugar is more nutritious than refined white sugar.

Evaporated cane juice: This is an unbleached, minimally processed alternative sweetener which is light in color and finely granulated. It can be substituted on a one-for-one basis for refined white sugar.

Organic Sucanat: Made from unrefined cane juice and is similar to pourable brown sugar in both color and appearance. This is a whole food and retains all of the vitamins and minerals found in nature. Wholesome Sweeteners is one brand and is found in health food stores and some supermarkets.

Organic sugar: Evaporated cane juice that is slightly refined and can be substituted one-for-one for refined white sugar in any recipe. Available at health food stores and some supermarkets.

Turbinado sugar: All-natural raw sugar obtained or crystallized from the initial pressing of sugar cane with no color, flavor or other additives. It may be used in the same way as white sugar. One teaspoon of turbinado sugar has 5 grams of carbohydrates and only 20 calories.

White sugar: Sugar that has been refined by bleaching and contains preservatives and additives.

Sweet Brown Rice (Mochi): This is another name for glutinous rice or sticky rice or sushi rice. Despite its name, this rice isn't sweet and it doesn't contain gluten. Instead, it's a very sticky, short-grain rice widely used by Asians who use it to make sushi and various desserts. You can buy it as either white or black (actually a rust color) rice.

Tamari: A wheat-free natural soy sauce with a mellow flavor that is widely available. Excellent for people with wheat allergies.

Tempeh: Fermented from whole soybeans, tempeh has more protein than tofu and has a richer flavor because it is made from the whole bean. Available in the refrigerated or freezer sections of health food stores and select supermarkets. Tempeh can be fried in a little oil, mixed with grains and vegetables in casseroles, and makes an excellent burger.

Tofu: Soybean curd made by coagulating soy milk with nigari (seaweed) or calcium chloride similar to the way cheese is made. Tofu is high in protein, low in saturated fats and cholesterol free. It can be used in many ways in many recipes.

Veggie Slices, Shreds and Toppings: A blend of organic soy, rice and oats resembling cheese slices and grated cheese. Soyco parmesan cheese topping, produced by the Galaxy Foods Company, is great on pizza!

Wheat Berries: Wheat kernels that have been stripped only of their inedible outer hulls. They're nutritious but take a long time to cook. Cracked wheat, bulgur or wheat flakes are good substitutes.

Wheat Germ: The innermost layer of a kernel of wheat, rich in vitamin E. Used in baked goods and other dishes to make them more nutritious. A good substitute is ground sunflower seeds.

Whole-Wheat Tortillas: Make sure the whole-wheat tortillas you purchase do not contain hydrogenated oil. This product is available widely.

Dr. William D. Stimack and Barbara Rolek

THE RECIPES

In the following recipes and throughout this book, you will see these symbols: * and †. Here is what they mean:

*See glossary of terms.
†Recipe provided elsewhere in this book.

Dr. William D. Stimack and Barbara Rolek

BREAKFAST
FOODS

Dr. William D. Stimack and Barbara Rolek

CREAMY OATMEAL

A high-fiber breakfast that's
hearty enough to give you energy all morning.

2 cups soy milk or vanilla soy milk*
1 cup old-fashioned rolled oats*
1/4 cup chopped raisins or dates
1/4 teaspoon cinnamon
Sprinkle of roasted nuts or seeds

- Place all ingredients in a saucepan. Bring to a boil. Cover (leaving lid ajar to prevent boiling over), reduce heat to very low and simmer for 10 minutes. Stir often. Serve topped with roasted nuts or seeds and fresh fruits of your choice.

Makes 2 servings. Each serving without nuts: 200 calories; 30 mg sodium; 0 mg cholesterol; 6 g fat; 52 g carbohydrate; 12 g protein; 9 g fiber.

Dr. William D. Stimack and Barbara Rolek

APRICOT SOFT RICE CEREAL

1 cup short-grain brown rice
1/8 teaspoon non-iodized sea salt
5 cups steam-distilled water
1/2 cup dried apricots, chopped

- Bring water and salt to a boil; add rice and apricots and return to the boil. Reduce heat, cover and simmer for 25 minutes, or until rice is tender. Portion into bowls and serve with soy or rice milk, if desired.

Makes 3 servings. Each serving: 285 calories; 103 mg sodium; 0 mg cholesterol; 1.8 g fat; 61.6 g carbohydrate; 5.6 g protein; 4.1 g fiber.

SWEET MILLET CEREAL

*Millet is a nutritious grain. This "pudding" can
be eaten for breakfast or as a dessert.*

Pudding:

1 cup raisins
2 cups steam-distilled water
1 cup uncooked millet*
1 cup raisin juice (see below)
1 cup steam-distilled water
1/8 teaspoon non-iodized sea salt
4 medium carrots, sliced

Sauce:

Soaked raisins
1 tablespoon arrowroot,* dissolved in 1 cup steam-distilled water
Pinch non-iodized sea salt
2 tablespoons barley malt syrup*
1/2 teaspoon pure vanilla
1/2 cup toasted almonds

- To make raisin juice, bring 1 cup raisins to boil in 2 cups water. Lower heat and simmer for about 15 minutes. Drain raisins, catching juices in a bowl. Reserve raisins for sauce and use juice in cooking millet.

- Bring millet, raisin juice, 1 cup water, salt and carrots to boil in a medium-sized saucepan. Lower heat, cover and simmer for 30 minutes. Purée hot millet mixture in food processor or blender and set aside.
- To prepare sauce, combine soaked raisins, dissolved arrowroot, salt, barley malt syrup, vanilla and almonds in small saucepan. Stir over medium heat until sauce thickens, about 5 minutes. Serve warm sauce over hot pudding.

Makes 4 servings: Each serving: 558 calories; 105 mg sodium; 0 mg cholesterol; 16.8 g fat; 88.1 g carbohydrate; 13.3 g protein; 10.8 g fiber.

TEMPEH AND POTATO SAUSAGES

Are eggs without sausage unthinkable?
Try this low-fat option instead.

2 tablespoons canola oil, plus additional oil for frying
8 ounces tempeh,* finely crumbled
1 small russet potato, grated
3 green onions, finely chopped
2 tablespoons arrowroot*
1 teaspoon dried sage
1 teaspoon dried thyme
1/4 teaspoon ground nutmeg
1/3 teaspoon ground black pepper
2 teaspoons tamari*
Sea salt to taste

- Preheat extra oil in skillet. In large bowl, combine all ingredients and mix well with your hands. Form mixture into eight 3/4" thick patties.
- Cook patties over medium heat on both sides until browned. Serve warm with organic eggs, any style.

Makes 4 servings. Each serving: 218 calories; 188 mg sodium; 0 mg cholesterol; 10 g fat; 21 g carbohydrate; 11 g protein.

HUEVOS RANCHEROS

Eggs Mexican style!

Spicy Fresh Tomato Sauce (recipe follows)
Refried Beans (recipe follows)
1 tablespoon olive oil
4 organic corn tortillas (6" in diameter)
4 organic eggs

- Make Spicy Fresh Tomato Sauce and Refried Beans and keep both warm.
- In a large skillet, heat 1/2 tablespoon oil over medium heat. Add tortillas, 1 or 2 at a time; cook 5 seconds per side, or until just soft, and remove to serving plates. Spread refried beans over tortillas.
- Add remaining 1/2 tablespoon oil to pan. Add eggs, 1 at a time, to pan and fry 3 minutes per side, or until cooked over easy. Place 1 fried egg on each serving of refried beans and top with tomato sauce. Serve hot.

Makes 4 servings. Each serving: 350 calories; 661 mg sodium; 211 mg cholesterol; 12 g fat; 40 g carbohydrate; 15 g protein; 9 g fiber.

Spicy Fresh Tomato Sauce:

1 teaspoon olive oil
1 small onion, minced
2 medium tomatoes, peeled and chopped
1/2 teaspoon non-iodized sea salt
1/8 teaspoon cayenne pepper
2 tablespoons chopped cilantro

- In skillet, heat oil over low heat. Add onion and cook, stirring frequently, 4 minutes, or until soft. Add tomatoes, salt and cayenne and cook, stirring frequently, 7 minutes, or until sauce is thick and dry. Remove pan from heat and stir in chopped cilantro.

Makes 1 cup. Each 1/4-cup serving: 23 calories; 299 mg sodium; 0 mg cholesterol; 1 g fat; 2.6 g carbohydrate; 0.4 g protein; 0.6 g fiber.

Refried Beans:

1 teaspoon olive oil
1 small onion, minced
1 garlic clove, minced
2 cups cooked pinto beans or organic canned beans, rinsed and drained
1/2 teaspoon non-iodized sea salt

- In skillet, heat oil over medium heat. Add onion and garlic and cook, stirring frequently, 4 minutes or until onion is tender. Add beans; mash lightly with potato masher until they are slightly lumpy; stir in salt. Cook, stirring frequently, 5 minutes, or until heated through.

Makes 2 cups. Each 1/2-cup serving: 136 calories; 297 mg sodium; 0 mg cholesterol; 1.5 g fat; 23.2 g carbohydrate; 7.2 g protein; 7.7 g fiber.

PANCAKES

1 to 2 tablespoons sunflower seeds (optional)
3/4 cup steam-distilled water (or half water and half soy milk*)
1/4 cup old-fashioned rolled oats*
1/4 of large apple, peeled and cut up
2/3 cup spelt flour (or whole-wheat pastry flour)*
1 rounded teaspoon baking power
1 teaspoon canola oil

- Place sunflower seeds in blender and process until finely ground. Add water, apple and oats and blend until apple is chopped. Add flour and baking powder and blend well. Oil hot griddle and portion batter out. Turn when edges start to brown. Top with pure maple syrup and fresh fruit, if desired.

Makes 3 servings. Each serving without sunflower seeds: 170 calories; 3 mg sodium; 0 mg cholesterol; 2.9 g fat; 30.2 g carbohydrate; 5.9 g protein; 4.9 g fiber.

Dr. William D. Stimack and Barbara Rolek

FRENCH TOAST

2 organic eggs, slightly beaten
1/2 cup apple juice
1 teaspoon ground cinnamon
1/4 teaspoon non-iodized sea salt
6 slices Natural Ovens bread (cinnamon-raisin is a good
  choice)
1 teaspoon canola oil
6 tablespoons pure maple syrup

- Beat together first four ingredients in a shallow pan. Add bread and soak for 2 minutes per side. Place on hot griddle that has been oiled with canola oil. Cook until golden brown.

Makes 3 servings. Each serving: 336 calories; 519 mg sodium; 142 mg cholesterol; 7.1 g fat; 58 g carbohydrate; 9.9 g protein; 3.6 g fiber.

MUFFINS
AND
QUICKBREADS

Dr. William D. Stimack and Barbara Rolek

BASIC MUFFINS

A low-sodium, zero-cholesterol muffin with
lots of possibilities.

1 cup oat bran*
3/4 cup whole-wheat flour
2 1/2 teaspoons low-sodium, aluminum-free baking
    powder
Dash non-iodized sea salt
Dash nutmeg
2 organic egg whites
1/4 cup honey
1/4 cup pineapple juice
1/3 cup olive oil
1/2 cup soy milk*

- Stir together oat bran, flour, baking powder, salt and nutmeg. Make a hole in center. Combine, egg whites, honey, juice, oil and milk. Add wet ingredients to dry all at once. Stir just until moistened. Batter will be lumpy. Place paper liners in a 12-cup muffin tin; fill 2/3 full. Bake at 375 F. for 20 to 25 minutes.

Makes 12 servings. Each serving: 143 calories; 30 mg sodium; 0 mg cholesterol; 6.9 g fat; 17.5 g carbohydrate; 2.7 g protein; 2.2 g fiber.

Dr. William D. Stimack and Barbara Rolek

Variations: Prepare muffins as directed above, but add:

3/4 cup blueberries OR
1 cup cranberries OR
1 cup apples and 1/4 cup raisins OR
1 cup mashed banana and 1/2 cup nuts (decrease honey to 1/8 cup)

BASIC OIL-FREE BRAN MUFFINS

Another muffin ready for your creativity.
It's very low in fat, low in sodium and has zero cholesterol.

2 1/4 cups oat bran*
1 tablespoon low-sodium, aluminum-free baking powder
1/4 cup Sucanat*
1/2 cup seedless raisins
1 1/4 cup soy or rice milk*
2 organic egg whites
2 tablespoons brown rice syrup*
1 teaspoon cinnamon

- Preheat oven to 425 F. Place paper liners in 12-cup muffin tin. Mix together dry ingredients in large bowl. In a separate bowl, mix together egg whites and syrup, and combine with dry ingredients. Don't overmix. Divide batter equally among cups. Bake 13 to 15 minutes or until toothpick comes out clean.

Note: For variety, substitute other dried fruits for raisins.

Makes 12 muffins. Each muffin: 132 calories; 22 mg sodium; 0 mg cholesterol; 1.2 g fat; 26.2 g carbohydrate; 4.1 g protein; 3.1 g fiber.

Dr. William D. Stimack and Barbara Rolek

NUTRI-MUFFINS

*This delicious recipe makes three dozen muffins
that are perfect as a nutritious school-class treat.
They freeze well for breakfast later on, too.*

1 cup whole-wheat flour*
1 cup organic unbleached white flour*
2/3 cup instant nonfat dry milk
1/2 cup Sucanat*
1/3 cup wheat germ*
2 teaspoons low-sodium, aluminum-free baking powder
1/2 teaspoon each non-iodized sea salt and baking soda
1/2 cup unsalted dry-roasted peanuts
1/4 cup walnuts (or pecans or almonds)
1/2 cup dried apricots
1/2 cup raisins
3 organic eggs
1/2 cup canola oil
1/3 cup molasses
2 bananas, mashed (or 1 cup grated carrots or zucchini)
3/4 cup orange juice

- Preheat oven to 350 F. Combine dry ingredients. Use food processor to chop nuts and apricots. Mix together dry ingredients, nuts, apricots and raisins in a large bowl. Blend thoroughly to prevent large lumps.
- Beat eggs in food processor until foamy. Add oil, molasses, orange juice and bananas in order given. Process after each addition. Pour liquid ingredients into dry ingredients. Mix

just until moistened. Grease muffin cups; fill 3/4 full with batter. Bake for 20 minutes.

Note: Batter can be baked in two greased 9"x5"x3" loaf pans for 1 hour or until toothpick comes out clean.

Makes 36 muffins. Each muffin: 127 calories; 64 mg sodium; 18 mg cholesterol; 5.1 g fat; 17.1 g carbohydrate; 2.9 g protein; 1.3 g fiber.

Dr. William D. Stimack and Barbara Rolek

MORNING GLORY MUFFINS

*A hearty muffin with a sweet taste
that will keep you going all morning long.*

1 cup soy milk*
3/4 cup bud-style bran cereal (such as Bran Buds, 100%
    Bran, Fiber-One)
1/2 cup golden raisins
1/2 cup shredded carrots
1 egg
1/3 cup honey
1/4 cup canola oil
1 teaspoon pure vanilla
1 1/4 cup whole-wheat flour
1 teaspoon baking soda
1 teaspoon ground cinnamon
1 tablespoon honey-crunch wheat germ (optional)

- Preheat oven to 425 F. Place paper liners in a 12-cup muffin tin. In a medium bowl, combine first eight ingredients. Let stand for 10 minutes.
- In a large bowl, combine flour, baking soda and cinnamon. Make a well in center and add milk mixture. Stir just until well combined. Don't overmix.
- Divide batter evenly among muffin cups. Sprinkle tops with wheat germ, if desired. Bake 15 to 20 minutes or until toothpick inserted in center comes out clean.

Makes 12 muffins. Each muffin: 164 calories; 131 mg sodium; 18 mg cholesterol; 6 g fat; 28 g carbohydrate; 4 g protein; 3 g fiber.

Dr. William D. Stimack and Barbara Rolek

CORN BREAD

*This is so easy, anyone in the family
can prepare it.*

3/4 cup stone-ground yellow cornmeal
1/4 cup whole-wheat pastry flour*
1/4 cup unbleached organic white flour*
1 tablespoon low-sodium, aluminum-free baking powder
1/4 teaspoon non-iodized sea salt
6 tablespoons canola oil
1 organic egg, beaten
1 cup soy milk*
1/3 cup pure maple syrup

- Preheat oven to 375 F. Mix together all dry ingredients. In separate bowl, mix wet ingredients. Stir wet into dry just until well combined. Place parchment circle in 9" baking pan and spoon in batter. Bake for 20 to 25 minutes or until golden brown. (These can also be made into muffins.)

Makes 8 servings. Each serving: 221 calories; 93 mg sodium; 26 mg cholesterol; 11.9 g fat; 24.9 g carbohydrate; 3.4 g protein; 1.8 g fiber.

BANANA BREAD

1 1/4 cup oat bran*
1/2 cup organic unbleached white flour*
1 1/4 teaspoons low-sodium, aluminum-free baking
   powder
1/2 teaspoon baking soda
1/3 cup honey
1/3 cup orange juice
1/3 cup canola oil
4 organic egg whites
2 mashed ripe bananas

- Preheat oven to 350 F. Stir together oat bran, flour, baking powder, baking soda and set aside. Beat honey, orange juice and oil until smooth. Add egg white ones at a time, beating until smooth. Line large loaf pan with parchment paper and pour in batter. Bake for 60 to 65 minutes or until toothpick comes out clean. Cool on wire rack for 15 minutes. Turn out and lay on side until cool.

Makes 12 servings. Each serving: 177 calories; 62 mg sodium; 35 mg cholesterol; 7.8 g fat; 23.7 g carbohydrate; 3.4 g protein; 2.1 g fiber.

PUMPKIN-ALMOND BREAD

1 cup white spelt flour*
3/4 cup ground almonds
1/2 teaspoon low-sodium, aluminum-free baking powder
1 teaspoon baking soda
1/2 teaspoon non-iodized sea salt
1/8 teaspoon cloves
1/2 teaspoon ginger
1/8 teaspoon nutmeg
3/4 cup turbinado sugar*
1/4 cup canola oil
2 organic eggs
1 cup organic canned unsweetened pumpkin
1/3 cup soy milk*
1/2 cup chopped dried figs or dates

- Preheat oven to 350 F. Grease a 9"x13" pan. Mix together flour, almonds, baking powder, baking soda, salt and spices. In separate bowl, beat sugar, oil and eggs until light. **Add** pumpkin and beat again.
- Quickly add dry ingredients, alternating with milk. Mix just until well combined. Add figs (or dates). Pour into prepared pan and bake 30 minutes or until toothpick comes out clean.

Makes 12 servings. Each serving: 228 calories; 265 mg sodium; 35 mg cholesterol; 10.2 g fat; 29.8 g carbohydrate; 4.2 g protein; 3.2 g fiber.

ZUCCHINI BREAD

3 organic eggs
1 cup sunflower or canola oil
3/4 cup turbinado sugar*
3/4 cup Sucanat*
1 tablespoon maple flavoring (not syrup)
2 cups zucchini, unpeeled and coarsely shredded
2 1/2 cups whole-wheat pastry flour*
1/2 cup raw wheat germ*
2 teaspoons baking soda
1 teaspoon non-iodized sea salt
1/2 teaspoon low-sodium, aluminum-free baking powder
1 cup nuts (pecans or walnuts), finely chopped
1/3 cup sesame seeds

- Preheat oven to 350 F. Beat eggs at high speed. With mixer running, slowly add oil, sugars and maple flavoring. Continue beating until thick and foamy. Stir in zucchini.
- In a separate bowl, combine flour, wheat germ, baking soda, salt, baking powder and nuts and stir gently into zucchini mixture. Divide batter equally between two large greased loaf pans. Sprinkle sesame seeds over tops. Bake for 1 hour or until toothpick comes out clean. Cool in pan 10 minutes. Turn out onto wire racks.

Makes 2 loaves (24 slices). Each slice: 246 calories; 215 mg sodium; 26 mg cholesterol; 14.2 g fat; 25 g carbohydrate; 4.3 g protein; 2.3 g fiber.

Dr. William D. Stimack and Barbara Rolek

SOUPS

Dr. William D. Stimack and Barbara Rolek

BASIC VEGETABLE STOCK

Excellent as a soup and
a flavorful base for almost any dish.

1 large onion
2 large carrots
2 celery ribs, including a few leaves (too many leaves and stock will be bitter)
1 bunch green onions, including half of the greens
8 garlic cloves, peeled and smashed
8 parsley sprigs
6 fresh thyme sprigs or 1/2 teaspoon dried
10 peppercorns
2 bay leaves
1 tablespoon olive or canola oil
2 quarts cold steam-distilled water
1/2 teaspoon non-iodized sea salt (or to taste)

- Chop vegetables into large chunks. You may peel the carrots if you like, but it's not necessary if they are well-washed. Heat oil in a soup pot. Add vegetables, garlic and herbs and cook over high heat for 5 to 10 minutes, stirring frequently. The more color they get, the more flavorful the stock will be. Add 1/2 teaspoon sea salt and 2 quarts cold water and bring to a boil. Lower the heat and simmer, uncovered, for 45 minutes. Strain, pressing on vegetables to release all the great flavor.

81

Note: If you want fragrance and complexity, add any combination of tomatoes, fennel, mushrooms, or other aromatic vegetable to the browning process, then boil and strain as above.

If you want a lighter broth, don't sauté the vegetables first. Just add all the ingredients to the pot. After the stock comes to a boil, simmer uncovered for 1 hour.

Makes 6 cups. Each cup: 66 calories; 238 mg sodium; 0 mg cholesterol; 2.5 g fat; 9.6 g carbohydrate; 1.7 g protein; 2.2 g fiber.

BASIC FISH STOCK

1 onion, chopped
1 carrot, chopped
1 rib celery with leaves, chopped
5 cups steam-distilled water
1 bay leaf
1 to 1 1/2 pounds skinless cold-water fish trimmings,
   bones or shrimp shells
Twist of lemon peel
1/4 teaspoon non-iodized salt
White pepper to taste

- Slowly bring all ingredients to a boil in a 2-quart pot, skimming when necessary. Partially cover and cook at medium for 20 to 30 minutes. Strain, pressing on ingredients to release the flavor.

Note: You may freeze the stock in ice cube trays, pop them into plastic bags and use as much or as little as you want at any time.

Makes 4 cups. Each 1/2-cup serving: 73 calories; 145 mg sodium; 17 mg cholesterol; 0.70 g fat; 3.8 g carbohydrate; 26 g protein; 2.2 g fiber.

Dr. William D. Stimack and Barbara Rolek

VEGETABLE CHOWDER

A low-fat, zero cholesterol soup, but watch the sodium and carbohydrates here if you need to.

1 tablespoon canola oil
1 small onion, diced
1 large celery rib, thinly sliced
1 large carrot, thinly sliced
1 clove garlic, finely diced
2 cups steam-distilled water
1 medium russet potato, peeled and diced
1/2 cup fresh or frozen corn
2 tablespoons tamari*
1 teaspoon dried basil
1 large bay leaf
1/4 teaspoon non-iodized sea salt
Pinch black pepper
2 ripe tomatoes, chopped
2 cups soy or rice milk

- In a 3-quart saucepan, sauté onions in oil until translucent. Add celery, carrots and garlic; sauté for several more minutes. Add water, potatoes, corn and seasonings; bring to a boil and then reduce heat to a simmer. Cover and cook for 15 minutes. Add tomatoes and simmer for 15 minutes longer. Add milk and adjust seasonings.

Makes 6 servings.   Each serving: 97 calories; 466 mg sodium; 0 mg cholesterol; 4.2 g fat; 11.2 g carbohydrate; 4.1 g protein; 2.6 g fiber.

Dr. William D. Stimack and Barbara Rolek

CORN CHOWDER

*A hearty bowl of soup without
all the fat and cholesterol.*

1 tablespoon canola oil
1/2 cup onion, diced
1/4 cup celery, thinly sliced
2 cups steam-distilled water
1 medium russet potato, peeled and diced
1 cup fresh or frozen corn
1/2 teaspoon non-iodized sea salt
1/4 teaspoon paprika
1 large bay leaf
2 cups soy or rice milk*
4 tablespoons organic pastry or unbleached white flour
Chopped parsley for garnish

- In a 3-quart saucepan, sauté onion and celery in oil until soft. Add water, potatoes, corn and seasonings. Bring to a boil and reduce to simmer. Cover with lid ajar and cook for 25 minutes. Add milk in which flour has been blended, stirring well. Simmer for 10 minutes. Adjust seasonings. Pour into bowls and garnish with parsley if desired.

Makes 6 servings. Each serving: 113 calories; 215 mg sodium; 0 mg cholesterol; 4.3 g fat; 14.9 g carbohydrate; 4 g protein; 2.5 g fiber.

CREAM OF POTATO SOUP

A low-calorie, zero cholesterol, low-sodium, low-fat soup.

2 tablespoons canola oil
1 large onion, diced
2 cups steam-distilled water
3 medium russet potatoes, thinly sliced
1 teaspoon dried parsley
1/2 teaspoon dried dill
1/4 teaspoon non-iodized sea salt
1/4 teaspoon black pepper
1 cup soy or rice milk
Chopped parsley for garnish

- In a small skillet, sauté onions in oil until they are translucent. Drain and add to a 3-quart saucepan with water, potatoes, herbs, salt and pepper. Bring to a boil; reduce to low and simmer 20 minutes or until potatoes are soft. Process soup in a blender until smooth. Return to low heat; add milk and adjust seasonings to taste. Pour into bowls and garnish with parsley.

Makes 6 servings. Each serving: 109 calories; 107 mg sodium; 0 mg cholesterol; 5.4 g fat; 12.4 g carbohydrate; 2.5 g protein; 1.9 g fiber.

Dr. William D. Stimack and Barbara Rolek

CREAM OF BROCCOLI AND YELLOW SQUASH SOUP

A cream soup with 0 milligrams cholesterol!

4 tablespoons olive oil
1 medium yellow onion, diced
2 garlic cloves, crushed
3 cups broccoli, chopped
2 cups yellow crookneck squash, sliced
1 large bay leaf
1/2 teaspoon non-iodized sea salt
2 1/2 cups vegetable stock†
2 cups soy or rice milk*
1/2 teaspoon dried basil
1/2 teaspoon dried thyme
1/2 teaspoon dried marjoram
1/8 teaspoon black pepper
1 cup broccoli florets
Chopped fresh chives for garnish

- In a 3-quart saucepan over medium heat, sauté onions and garlic in oil until soft and translucent. Add 3 cups broccoli, squash, bay leaf, salt and stock. Cover and cook for 15 minutes or until broccoli is tender. Purée mixture in blender or food processor until smooth and creamy. Return to pot, whisk in milk and seasonings and simmer over low for 10 minutes. Steam broccoli florets 3 to 5 minutes; add to soup. Serve with chopped chives for garnish.

Makes 6 servings. Each serving: 135 calories; 323 mg sodium; 0 mg cholesterol; 7.5 g fat; 12.2 g carbohydrate; 5.2 g protein; 4.8 g fiber.

Dr. William D. Stimack and Barbara Rolek

CREAM OF MUSHROOM SOUP

A bowl of soup and a leafy green salad make a hearty lunch.

2 teaspoons canola oil
1 medium onion, diced
1 cup celery, thinly sliced
15 to 20 button mushrooms, washed
2 cups White Sauce†
1/4 teaspoon dry mustard
1/4 teaspoon black pepper
2 1/4 cups soy or rice milk*

- In 3-quart saucepan over medium heat, sauté onion in oil for 2 to 3 minutes. Add celery and whole mushrooms. Cook until mushrooms release some of their moisture. Reduce heat, cover and simmer 20 minutes. Meanwhile, make recipe for White Sauce.
- Place sautéed vegetables in food processor with White Sauce. Purée until creamy. Return to heat; add dry mustard, pepper and milk. Simmer for 5 to 8 minutes. Adjust seasonings. If too thick, add up to 1 cup vegetable stock for a thinner consistency.

Makes 6 servings. Each serving: 213 calories; 254 mg sodium; 0 mg cholesterol; 13.7 g fat; 15.3 g carbohydrate; 6.8 g protein; 4.6 g fiber.

MEXICAN BLACK BEAN SOUP

High in protein and fiber. If you cook your own beans,
you won't have to worry about the sodium, either.
Olé!

2 tablespoons canola oil
2 medium onions, chopped
4 medium garlic cloves, minced
1 small jalapeño chile, stemmed and minced (remove seeds if you like)
1 tablespoon ground cumin
1 tablespoon chili powder
2 1/2 cups steam-distilled water
5 (15-ounce) cans organic black beans, drained and rinsed
2 tablespoons lime juice
Soy sour cream*
4 teaspoons minced fresh cilantro leaves

- Heat oil in large saucepan. Add onions and sauté over medium heat until translucent, about 5 minutes. Stir in garlic and jalapeño and cook until garlic is golden, about 1 minute.
- Add cumin and chili powder and cook, stirring frequently, until spices are fragrant, about 1 minute. Pour water into pot. Bring to a boil and simmer about 3 minutes.
- Add beans and bring back to a boil. Remove 2 cups of broth and beans and purée in blender. Return to pot. Stir in lime juice, reheating if necessary.

Dr. William D. Stimack and Barbara Rolek

- Ladle soup into individual bowls. Swirl soy sour cream into bowls and sprinkle with cilantro. Serve immediately.

Makes 4 to 6 servings. Each serving: 335 calories; 486 mg sodium; 6 g fat; 50 g carbohydrate; 18 g protein; 15 g fiber.

BUTTERNUT SQUASH SOUP

A beautiful color and velvety smooth with the crunch of toasted pumpkin seeds.

1 butternut squash, about 1 1/2 pounds, cut in half lengthwise and seeded
1 tablespoon olive oil
1 medium onion, sliced
1 teaspoon freshly ground black pepper
6 cups vegetable stock†
1 lime for garnish, cut into eighths
Toasted pumpkin seeds for garnish (recipe follows)

- Preheat oven to 450 F. Bake squash, cut-side down in a parchment-lined roasting pan with 1 inch of water until soft, 45 to 60 minutes. When cool enough to handle, scrape out interior flesh and reserve.
- Heat olive oil over moderate heat in large stockpot. Sauté onions with pinch of salt and pepper until golden, 10 to 15 minutes. Add squash and stock. Bring to a boil, reduce and simmer uncovered for 10 minutes.
- Purée in a blender until smooth. Strain back into pot and add more stock if too thick. Return to a boil and remove from heat. Serve in heated bowls with a wedge of lime squeezed over each bowl and dropped in; add a sprinkling of pepita seeds.

Toasted Pepitas: In a small, dry frying pan set over medium heat, toast 1 cup pumpkin seeds until golden brown, 3 to 5

93

minutes. Turn the heat off. Add 1/4 cup lime juice mixed with 1/4 teaspoon sea salt and shake the pan vigorously. Cook, shaking often, until the pan is dry and cool.

Makes 6 servings. Each serving: 217 calories; 341 mg sodium; 0 mg cholesterol; 6.8 g fat; 33.2 g carbohydrate; 5.9 g protein; 4.4 g fiber.

ITALIAN CHICKPEAS AND RICE SOUP

Keep your refrigerator stocked with this
filling soup for a great pick-me-up anytime of the day.

2 teaspoons olive oil
1 large onion, finely diced
5 cloves garlic, minced
3 (15-ounce) cans low-sodium organic chickpeas, undrained
12 cups vegetable stock†
1/3 cup tomato sauce†
1 (8-ounce) package organic Italian-flavored risotto
Dried or fresh basil, oregano and flat-leaf parsley to taste

- Sauté onion, garlic and olive oil in large soup pot. Add chickpeas, stock, and tomato sauce. When soup comes to a boil, add risotto. Cook, uncovered until rice is tender. Adjust seasonings.

Makes 16 servings. Each 1-cup serving: 235 calories; 215 mg sodium; 0 mg cholesterol; 4.3 g fat; 40 g carbohydrate; 8.9 g protein; 7.6 g fiber.

Dr. William D. Stimack and Barbara Rolek

ASIAN MUSHROOM-MISO SOUP WITH WATERCRESS

This broth features the healing powers of shiitake and enoki mushrooms, ginger and garlic.

2 1/2 teaspoons dark sesame oil
8 ounces shiitake mushrooms, stems discarded, caps sliced thin
1 medium onion, halved and sliced thin
5 cups vegetable stock†
6 tablespoons mild white miso*
1 (1-inch) piece peeled fresh gingerroot
6 garlic cloves, peeled
1 large bunch watercress, tough stems removed, coarsely chopped
1 (3.5-ounce) package enoki mushrooms, separated, root ends trimmed

- Heat oil in soup pot over medium heat. Add shiitake mushrooms and onion and sauté until softened, about 5 minutes. Stir in stock and miso; bring just to a boil.
- Combine gingerroot and garlic in food processor with metal blade. Pulse until minced. Add to simmering soup. Stir in watercress and enoki mushrooms and cook until greens wilt and mushrooms look puffy and white, about 2 minutes. Serve immediately.

Makes 4 servings. Each serving: 248 calories; 688 mg sodium; 5 g fat; 48 g carbohydrate; 9 g protein; 8 g fiber.

GINGER-CARROT SOUP

Clean Asian flavors in a creamy broth.

4 tablespoons coriander seeds
1 tablespoon canola oil
2 large onions, sliced
2 cloves garlic, minced
2 teaspoons minced fresh ginger
2 pounds sliced carrots
9 cups vegetable stock†
1/2 teaspoon freshly ground black pepper
1/2 cup soy sour cream* for garnish

- In a dry skillet over medium-high heat, toast coriander seeds until golden, about 3 minutes, shaking constantly until fragrant. Cool and process in a blender or mortar and pestle to a fine powder. Reserve.
- In large saucepan over high heat, warm oil. Add onions and cook for 3 minutes, stirring occasionally, until translucent. Add garlic, ginger, carrots, stock, salt, pepper and ground coriander. Bring to a boil. Reduce heat; cover and simmer for 45 minutes or until carrots are tender.
- Process in a blender until smooth. Portion out soup, garnishing with a dollop of sour cream.

Makes 8 servings. Each serving: 214 calories; 386 mg sodium; 4 mg cholesterol; 7.9 g fat; 31.3 g carbohydrate; 4.1 g protein; 7.9 g fiber.

Dr. William D. Stimack and Barbara Rolek

SALADS
AND
DRESSINGS

Dr. William D. Stimack and Barbara Rolek

FRESH VEGETABLE SALAD
WITH HONEY-MUSTARD DRESSING

This colorful salad is easy to make,
low in fat and full of flavor!

Salad:

4 cups torn spinach leaves
1 cup chopped cauliflower
1 cup shredded red cabbage
1/2 cup sliced fresh mushrooms
1/2 cup sliced radishes

Honey-Mustard Dressing:

2 tablespoons Nayonaise*
1 to 2 tablespoons Dijon mustard
2 tablespoons honey
1 tablespoon tarragon vinegar

- In large bowl, combine all salad ingredients and toss gently. In small bowl, using wire whisk, combine all dressing ingredients; blend well. Pour dressing over salad; toss gently. If desired, sprinkle with coarsely ground black pepper. Serve immediately.

Makes 5 servings. Each 1-cup serving: 70 calories; 270 mg sodium; 0 mg cholesterol; 1 g fat; 13 g carbohydrate; 3 g protein; 2 g fiber.

Dr. William D. Stimack and Barbara Rolek

GRAPE AND BROCCOLI SLAW

A new take on a familiar theme.

Salad:

4 cups broccoli stems, julienned
2 cups seedless grapes, halved
1 (16-ounce) can organic navy beans, rinsed and drained
1/2 cup sliced water chestnuts
1/2 cup balsamic dressing (recipe follows)
1 cup shredded cheddar-flavored soy cheese

Dressing:

1/3 cup balsamic vinegar
2 tablespoons olive oil
2 tablespoons Dijon-style mustard
1 tablespoon chopped fresh basil
1/2 teaspoon non-iodized sea salt
1/4 teaspoon freshly ground pepper

- Toss broccoli stems, grapes, beans, and water chestnuts together. Blend dressing ingredients well and toss with salad mixture. Refrigerate until serving time. Mix in cheese and serve.

Makes 4 servings. Each serving: 335 calories; 674 mg sodium; 16 mg cholesterol; 12 g fat; 45 g carbohydrate; 19 g protein.

ASPARAGUS, POTATO AND PAPAYA SALAD WITH GREEN-ONION DRESSING

*This colorful salad is hearty enough
for a main course.*

Salad:

> 1 pound asparagus
> 1 pound thin-skinned red potatoes, scrubbed
> 1 firm-ripe papaya (about 1 pound), peeled and seeded
> 4 cups mixed salad greens
> 1/2 cup kalamata olives, pitted
> Non-iodized sea salt

- Snap off and discard tough asparagus ends. In a large pan over high heat, bring 2 quarts water to a boil. Add asparagus, cook until barely tender, 3 to 5 minutes. Remove asparagus with tongs and shock in ice water. When cool, about 3 minutes, lift out and drain.
- Meanwhile, add potatoes to same pot of boiling water. Cover and simmer over medium heat until they are just tender when pierced with a knife, 20 to 30 minutes. Drain and shock in ice water. When cool, about 10 minutes, drain and cut into halves. Cut papaya lengthwise into 1/4-inch thick slices.
- Line a platter with salad mix. Arrange asparagus, potatoes, papaya, and olives on greens. Add dressing and salt to taste to individual portions.

Makes 4 servings. Each serving: 296 calories; 807 mg sodium; 0 mg cholesterol; 12 g fat; 46 g carbohydrate; 7 g protein; 5 g fiber.

Dressing:

8 green onions
1/4 cup seasoned rice vinegar
2 tablespoons Dijon mustard
2 tablespoons canola oil
2 tablespoons vegetable stock†
Chopped fresh parsley
Chopped fresh mint
Chopped fresh basil leaves
White pepper to taste

- Rinse and trim ends from green onions; cut into 2-inch pieces (including tops). Purée all ingredients until smooth. Stir in white pepper to taste.

Makes 1 cup. Each tablespoon: 24 calories; 121 mg sodium; 0 mg cholesterol; 2 g fat; 1 g carbohydrate; 0.2 g protein; 0.3 g fiber.

FRUIT AND GREENS

Wonderful with broiled fish.

Dressing:

>   2/3 cup organic low-fat, low-sodium Italian dressing
>   1/2 cup orange juice

Salad:

>   3 cups torn spinach leaves
>   3 cups torn romaine lettuce leaves
>   2 oranges, peeled, sectioned
>   2 avocados, peeled, sliced
>   1 cup sliced strawberries

*   In small bowl, combine dressing ingredients, blending well. In large bowl, combine all salad ingredients. Pour dressing over salad, tossing well to coat. Serve immediately.

Makes 8 servings. Each serving: 290 calories; 50 mg sodium; 0 mg cholesterol; 26 g fat; 12 g carbohydrate; 2 g protein; 5 g fiber.

Dr. William D. Stimack and Barbara Rolek

PIÑA COLADA CARROT-RAISIN SALAD

A refreshing taste of the islands.

1 cup pineapple or orange juice
1 cup Sucanat*
1 cup raisins
1 cup shredded, unsweetened coconut
6 ounces soy or rice milk
2 pounds shredded carrots

- In a medium-size saucepan, combine juice and Sucanat. Bring to a boil, stirring to dissolve Sucanat. Remove from heat. Add raisins, coconut and soy milk. Mix well and cool. When mixture is cool, add carrots. Refrigerate until completely cold.

Makes 6 servings. Each serving: 398 calories; 63 mg sodium; 0 cholesterol; 11 g fat; 78 g carbohydrate; 4 g protein; 7 g fiber.

JICAMA SALAD

Jicama, also called the Mexican potato,
has a sweet, nutty flavor.

1/2 cup soy sour cream*
2 tablespoons lime juice
2 tablespoons chopped fresh cilantro or 2 teaspoons dried
1/2 teaspoon ground cumin
1/4 teaspoon non-iodized sea salt
1/4 teaspoon black pepper
1 pound jicama, julienned
1 small cucumber, peeled, seeded, julienned
1 medium carrot, julienned
Radicchio

- In medium bowl, stir together soy sour cream, lime juice, cilantro, cumin, salt and pepper. Toss with jicama, cucumber and carrot. Serve on a bed of radicchio, if desired.

Makes 4 servings. Each serving: 82 calories; 168 mg sodium; 2 mg cholesterol; 1 g fat; 16 g carbohydrate; 4 g protein.

EGGLESS EGG SALAD

A low-fat, low-cholesterol version of the original.

1/2 cup Nayonaise*
2 tablespoons Dijon mustard
1/2 teaspoon non-iodized sea salt
1/2 teaspoon white pepper
1 teaspoon turmeric
1 pound firm tofu, drained and pressed (see "Before You
    Start Cooking")
1/2 cup chopped red onions
1/2 cup chopped celery
1 teaspoon honey
2 tablespoons capers (optional)
1 teaspoon fresh dill or 2 teaspoons dried
1/2 teaspoon freshly ground black pepper

- Mix together all ingredients except tofu until well blended.
  Crumble tofu and toss in, cover and chill.

Makes 6 servings. Each serving: 107 calories; 416 mg
sodium; 5 mg cholesterol; 5.8 g fat; 7.7 g carbohydrate; 5.7 g
protein; 0.6 g fiber.

TOFU WALDORF SALAD

The addition of tofu makes this a main-course salad.

2 ounces dried cherries
2 ounces fresh orange juice
2 ounces walnuts, coarsely chopped
1 celery rib, diced
1 Granny Smith apple, skin-on, diced
2/3 cup Nayonaise*
2/3 cup soy sour cream*
1 teaspoon turbinado sugar*
1 pound firm tofu, drained and pressed (see "Before You
    Start Cooking")
1 ounce blanched sliced almonds for garnish
1 chopped green onion, for garnish

- Soak dried cherries in orange juice for 1/2 hour. Drain and reserve juice. In large bowl, toss together cherries, walnuts, celery and apples. Pour reserved orange juice over all.
- In a separate bowl, mix Nayonaise, sour cream and sugar. Drain apple mixture and combine with dressing. Dice tofu and lightly toss in. Add sea salt if necessary. Chill.
- For a main course dish, place salad on a bed of leaf lettuce with orange slices, grapes and melon slices. Sprinkle with almonds and sliced green onions.

Makes 4 servings: Each serving: 412 calories; 271 mg sodium; 10 mg cholesterol; 23.6 g fat; 37.3 g carbohydrate; 12.5 g protein; 4.3 g fiber.

Dr. William D. Stimack and Barbara Rolek

GARDEN BOW-TIE SALAD

*Everything but the kitchen sink dressed
in an Italian vinaigrette.*

1 pound organic bow-tie pasta
1 cup thinly sliced red onion
1/2 green pepper, diced
1/2 red pepper, diced
1 cup shredded carrots
1 cucumber, unpeeled (if not waxed) and cut 1/4"
1 pint cherry tomatoes
8 ounces low-fat, low-sodium Italian dressing
Non-iodized sea salt and freshly ground black pepper to
taste

- Cook pasta al dente; shock in cold water and drain. In a large bowl, combine all ingredients, adding more dressing if needed, and adjusting seasonings.

Makes 8 servings. Each serving: 375 calories; 238 mg sodium; 0 mg cholesterol; 14.7 g fat; 52.2 g carbohydrate; 8.5 g protein; 3.2 g fiber.

NUTTY DRESSING

*This versatile dressing can be
used in many ways.*

1/2 cup chopped walnuts
1/2 cup extra-virgin olive oil
1/4 cup balsamic vinegar
1/4 cup orange juice
1/2 teaspoon non-iodized sea salt, or to taste

- Put all ingredients in a food processor and blend to desired smoothness.

Makes 1 1/4 cups. Each 2-tablespoon serving: 138 calories; 117 mg sodium; 15 g fat; 2 g carbohydrate; 1 g protein.

Note: For a green salad, toss with a variety of greens, chunky raw vegetables and chickpeas. For cole slaw, toss with shredded cabbage and mandarin oranges. Use as a sauce with hot or cold steamed vegetables or fish such as salmon or swordfish.

Dr. William D. Stimack and Barbara Rolek

CREAMY CILANTRO-SESAME DRESSING

This versatile dressing is great as a dip, spread, or as an accompaniment for broiled fish.

4 ounces silken or soft tofu, well drained
1/2 jalapeño, seeded and chopped
Zest and juice of 1/2 large lime
3 tablespoons soy sour cream*
1 teaspoon toasted sesame oil
1/2 cup fresh cilantro leaves, coarsely chopped
1 green onion, including 1" of green portion, sliced
non-iodized sea salt
White pepper
2 teaspoons snipped chives

- Combine first five ingredients in small food processor and purée until smooth, stopping several times to scrape down sides. Add cilantro and green onion and purée just enough to make a flecked pale green sauce. Taste and season with salt and pepper. Scrape into serving bowl and sprinkle with chives.

Makes 3/4 cup. Each tablespoon: 25 calories; 28 mg sodium; 1 mg cholesterol; 2 g fat; 1 g carbohydrate; 2 g protein; 1 g fiber.

TOASTED SESAME DRESSING

This is terrific tossed on pasta or on slivered napa cabbage,
pea pods, cucumbers and radishes.

1 tablespoon minced gingerroot
1 large clove garlic, minced
1 large jalapeño, seeded and chopped
4 teaspoons sesame tahini*
1 tablespoon dark sesame oil
1 tablespoon light sesame oil or canola oil
1 tablespoon tamari*
2 tablespoons rice vinegar
1/2 teaspoon Sucanat*
3 tablespoons chopped cilantro
3 tablespoons chopped basil
1 tablespoon chopped mint
1 tablespoon toasted black and/or white sesame seeds
Non-iodized sea salt to taste

- Purée ginger, garlic jalapeño, tahini, oils, tamari, vinegar and Sucanat in small food processor or blender until smooth. Add cilantro, basil and mint and pulse briefly. Add sesame seeds and salt, if necessary. Chill.

Makes 4 servings. Each 2-tablespoon serving: 122 calories; 254 mg sodium; 0 mg cholesterol; 10.6 g fat; 4.5 g carbohydrate; 2.2 g protein; fiber 1.3 g.

CINNAMON-HONEY DRESSING

Great on tossed salads and as a fruit dip.

3/4 cup vanilla soy milk*
1 package (12 ounces) firm silken tofu*
2 tablespoons honey
2 teaspoons pure vanilla
2 teaspoons ground cinnamon
1 tablespoon lemon juice

- Place all ingredients in blender or food processor and mix well. Store in refrigerator. Serve over fresh fruit or tossed lettuce salad. It also makes a delicious dip for fresh fruits.

Makes 2 cups. Each 2-tablespoon serving: 30 calories; 19 mg sodium; 0 mg cholesterol; 0.5 g fat; 4 g carbohydrate; 2 g protein.

GINGER VINAIGRETTE

A clean taste with a little bite.

1/2 cup canola oil
1/2 cup rice vinegar
1 teaspoon turbinado sugar*
1 teaspoon finely chopped fresh ginger
1/2 teaspoon non-iodized sea salt

- Mix all ingredients and drizzle over mixed greens.

Makes 1 cup: Each 2-tablespoon serving: 129 calories; 147 mg sodium; 0 mg cholesterol; 13.6 g fat; 1.4 g carbohydrate; 0 g protein; 0 g fiber.

Dr. William D. Stimack and Barbara Rolek

PASTAS
AND
SAUCES

Dr. William D. Stimack and Barbara Rolek

SPINACH FETTUCCINE WITH "MEAT" SAUCE

*Tempeh replaces the meat in this recipe
that's as Italian as they come.*

1 large yellow onion, finely diced
1 stalk celery, finely diced
1 carrot, peeled and grated
4 cloves garlic, minced
2 to 3 tablespoons olive oil
3/4 teaspoon dried thyme
3/4 teaspoon ground fennel seed
1/2 teaspoon dried oregano
1/4 teaspoon non-iodized sea salt, or to taste
1 teaspoon fresh rosemary, minced (or 1/2 teaspoon dried)
1 (8-ounce) package marinated tempeh,* finely crumbled
3/4 cup vegetable stock†
1 (28-ounce) can organic tomato purée
1/2 teaspoon ground pepper
1/4 cup minced fresh basil
Parmesan-flavored soy cheese topping
12 ounces organic spinach fettuccine

- In large pan, sauté onion, celery, carrot and garlic in olive oil until onion is soft and slightly browned. Add thyme, fennel, oregano, salt and rosemary. Stir in crumbled tempeh and sauté for 5 additional minutes.

- Add stock and tomatoes; cover and simmer for 20 to 30 minutes. Uncover and a cook a few more minutes to thicken, adding pepper and fresh basil. Set aside and keep warm.
- In large pot of salted boiling water, cook pasta until al dente. Drain and toss with sauce. Garnish with parmesan.

Makes 6 servings. Each serving: 427 calories; 628 mg sodium; 4 mg cholesterol; 11 g fat; 67 g carbohydrate; 19 g protein.

FETTUCCINE PRIMAVERA WITH WHITE SAUCE

2 tablespoons extra-virgin olive oil
2 cloves garlic, minced
1 head broccoli, thinly sliced
1 large red pepper, thinly sliced
10 large mushrooms, thinly sliced
1 small red onion, sliced
1 cup frozen baby peas, thawed
1/2 cup fresh basil, cut into strips
1/2 cup black olives, sliced
12 ounces whole-wheat fettuccine
3 cups white sauce†
2 tablespoons parmesan-flavored soy topping*

- In a medium pan, sauté garlic and broccoli in oil for 5 minutes. Add peppers, mushrooms and onions, and sauté over medium heat for 5 to 10 more minutes. Stir in peas and warm through. Add basil and olives; cover and set aside.
- Cook pasta following package directions. Serve immediately topped with sautéed vegetables and a generous portion of white sauce. Top with parmesan.

Makes 4 servings. Each serving: 460 calories; 593 mg sodium; 2 mg cholesterol; 26.3 g fat; 42.3 g carbohydrate; 13.2 g protein; 11.8 g fiber.

Dr. William D. Stimack and Barbara Rolek

LINGUINE WITH ASPARAGUS AND SAFFRON-TOMATO SAUCE

Red, yellow and green are pretty on the plate.
High in carbohydrates, fiber and protein;
low in sodium and fat.

3/4 pound medium asparagus
1 tablespoon extra-virgin olive oil
1 medium onion, chopped fine
1/4 teaspoon saffron threads
1/2 cup vegetable stock†
1 (14.5-ounce) can organic diced tomatoes
Non-iodized sea salt and freshly ground black pepper
1 pound whole-wheat or spinach linguine

- Bring 4 quarts water to a boil in a large pot. Meanwhile, snap off tough ends of asparagus, halve spears lengthwise and cut them diagonally into 1-inch pieces.
- Heat oil in large skillet. Add onion and cook over medium heat until golden, about 4 minutes. Stir in saffron and stock; bring to boil and cook for 1 minute. Stir in tomatoes and simmer until sauce thickens slightly, about 5 minutes. Season with salt and pepper to taste.
- Meanwhile, add pasta and salt to taste to boiling water. Cook until almost al dente. Add asparagus and cook until asparagus is tender, about 2 more minutes. Drain and toss pasta and asparagus with tomato sauce. Serve immediately.

Makes 6 servings. Each serving: 277 calories; 121 mg sodium; 0 mg cholesterol; 3.5 g fat; 50.3 g carbohydrate; 10.9 g protein; 9.5 g fiber.

SPINACH LASAGNA

*No one will believe that the cheesy, herbed filling
is really tofu, and you don't have to cook the noodles first!*

8 ounces whole-wheat or spelt lasagna noodles
32-ounce jar organic spaghetti sauce (70 calories or less
   per 1/2-cup serving)
1 1/2 cups steam-distilled water

Filling:

1 pound soft or medium tofu, drained
1 (10-ounce) package frozen, chopped spinach thawed
   and drained well
1 teaspoon dried oregano
1/2 teaspoon dried basil
1/8 teaspoon garlic powder

- Preheat oven to 350 F. In large bowl, combine sauce and water; set aside. Drain tofu slightly, but do not squeeze out the water. Place in a blender and process until smooth. Spoon into a bowl, add remaining filling ingredients and mix well.
- To assemble, spread 1 cup of sauce in bottom of a 9"x13" glass pan. Top with 1/3 noodles and 1/2 cup sauce. Spoon 1/2 of tofu mixture over noodles and top with another 1/2 cup sauce. Top with another 1/3 noodles and press down firmly. Repeat layers, adding 1/2 cup sauce, remaining tofu mixture, 1/2 cup sauce and remaining noodles.

- Spoon remaining sauce over noodles, making sure noodles are entirely covered. Bake 40 minutes, covered. Uncover and continue to bake 20 more minutes. Cut into squares to serve.

Makes 6 servings. Each serving: 324 calories; 720 mg sodium; 0 mg cholesterol; 8.4 g fat; 48.6 g carbohydrate; 13.3 g protein; 9.6 g fiber.

Dr. William D. Stimack and Barbara Rolek

VEGETABLE LASAGNA

*Vary the vegetables with the season and
with your whim!*

8 ounces whole-wheat, spelt or spinach lasagna noodles
1 teaspoon olive oil
1 medium onion, chopped
2 cloves garlic, minced
2 cups medium tofu,* drained but not pressed
1/4 cup parmesan-flavored soy topping*
2 tablespoons dried parsley
2 (15-ounce) jars organic pasta sauce
1 medium zucchini, chopped
1 cup broccoli, chopped
1 cup mushrooms, sliced
8 ounces grated mozzarella-flavored soy cheese
10-ounce package frozen, chopped spinach, thawed

- Preheat oven to 375 F. Cook pasta al dente. Sauté onion and garlic in oil until translucent. In a bowl, mix tofu, parmesan and parsley. Lightly oil a 9"x13" glass dish. In a separate bowl, mix pasta sauce with zucchini, broccoli, mushrooms, and sautéed onions and garlic.
- Place 1/2 of noodles in prepared baking dish. Top with 1/2 of tofu mixture, 1/2 of pasta sauce and 1/2 of mozzarella cheese. Top with all of the spinach. Repeat layers. Bake 30 to 40 minutes or until bubbly.

Makes 8 servings. Each serving: 289 calories; 553 mg sodium; 2 mg cholesterol; 9.1 g fat; 39.7 g carbohydrate; 11.7 g protein; 7.2 g fiber.

Dr. William D. Stimack and Barbara Rolek

SPINACH PARSLEY PESTO

A healthier spin on the original.

2 cloves garlic
1 bunch flat-leaf parsley (about 1 cup packed leaves)
2 cups packed spinach leaves, about 5 ounces
1/3 cup extra-virgin olive oil
1/2 cup pine nuts (pignoli)
1/2 cup parmesan-flavored soy topping*
1/8 teaspoon non-iodized sea salt

- Drop peeled garlic cloves into feed tube of food processor and chop finely. Rinse and dry the parsley; remove and discard tough stems. Drop leaves into feed tube and mince finely.
- Wash spinach, removing any tough stems and discard. Add half to processor bowl and drizzle a tablespoon of oil through feed tube while processing until finely minced, about 15 seconds. Repeat with remaining spinach and oil. Add pine nuts and process until well-chopped, about 15 seconds.
- Add parmesan-flavored soy topping and salt to bowl while drizzling remaining oil through feed tube, about 15 seconds. Serve at once on pasta or pizza. Refrigerate up to 4 days, or freeze up to 3 months.

Makes 1 1/2 cups. Each teaspoon: 19 calories; 20 mg sodium; 1 mg cholesterol; 2 g fat; 0 g carbohydrate; 1 g protein; 0 g fiber.

ALFREDO SAUCE

All the flavor of the original without the fat!

12 ounces soft tofu, drained
1 teaspoon minced garlic
1/2 cup parmesan-flavored soy topping*
1 tablespoon olive oil
1 1/2 teaspoons dried basil
1 tablespoon dried parsley
1/4 teaspoon black pepper
1 teaspoon onion powder

- Combine all ingredients in food processor. Blend on high speed 1 1/2 minutes, until creamy. Heat sauce in microwave or stove top and serve over hot pasta.

Makes 4 servings. Each 1/2 cup: 125 calories; 5 g fat; 4 g carbohydrate; 9 g protein.

Dr. William D. Stimack and Barbara Rolek

SIMPLE TOMATO SAUCE

*This quick sauce takes only
30 minutes to prepare.*

3 tablespoons extra-virgin olive oil
3 garlic cloves, minced
1 can (28 ounces) organic crushed tomatoes
Cracked black pepper and non-iodized sea salt
2 tablespoons minced fresh parsley

- In a large saucepan, heat garlic and oil over medium-high heat until garlic starts to sizzle. Stir in tomatoes and bring to a simmer; continue to simmer over medium-low heat until sauce thickens and flavors meld, about 10 to 15 minutes. Taste and adjust seasonings. Stir in parsley.

Makes 4 servings. Each serving: 130 calories; 295 mg sodium; 0 mg cholesterol; 10 g fat; 10 g carbohydrate; 2 g protein; 2 g fiber.

WHITE SAUCE

This bechamel sauce can turn any ho-hum
dish into a gourmet delight!

4 tablespoons olive oil or organic butter
1 small yellow onion, finely chopped
1 clove garlic, minced
6 tablespoons wheat or brown rice flour*
1 cup soy or rice milk*
1/2 cup vegetable stock†
1/2 teaspoon non-iodized sea salt
Pinch white pepper

- In a heavy saucepan over low heat, sauté onion and garlic in oil or butter until soft and translucent. Sprinkle in flour and stir frequently for 5 minutes to make a roux. Slowly add milk, stock and seasonings, whisking vigorously. Increase heat and allow to come to a boil. Reduce heat to low and simmer for 5 minutes, stirring often. Adjust seasonings and thickness by adding more water or flour in small increments. Best served immediately or allow to cool and refrigerate for later use.

Note: For Indian cuisine, add 1 teaspoon curry powder; for an Italian flair, add 1/4 teaspoon each of powdered garlic, dried basil and oregano; as a cream sauce for fish, add 1 teaspoon dried dill, 3 tablespoons lemon juice and 2 tablespoons capers.

131

Dr. William D. Stimack and Barbara Rolek

Makes 2 cups. Each 1/4-cup serving: 199 calories; 333 mg sodium; 0 mg cholesterol; 15.2 g fat; 11.7 g carbohydrate; 3.6 g protein; 2.8 g fiber.

HERBED GRAVY

2 tablespoons canola oil
1/3 cup whole-wheat pastry flour*
1 cup soy or rice milk*
1 tablespoon tamari*
1 cup vegetable stock†
1/4 teaspoon non-iodized sea salt
1 teaspoon dried, crushed sage
1/4 teaspoon dried thyme
1/4 teaspoon dried marjoram
Pinch black pepper

- In a 2-quart saucepan over medium heat, heat oil and add flour; stir often for 2 minutes. Remove from heat and allow to cool for several minutes. In a separate bowl, combine remaining ingredients. Whisk with flour-oil mixture, half at a time to avoid lumping. Return to medium heat and bring to boil, stirring often. Reduce to low and cook for 10 to 15 minutes, stirring occasionally. If gravy seems too thick, whisk in additional stock, 1 tablespoon at a time until desired consistency is reached. Adjust seasonings. Gravy will thicken as it cools. Stores well in refrigerator for several days.

Note: For mushroom gravy, add sautéed mushrooms and onions when gravy is simmering.

Dr. William D. Stimack and Barbara Rolek

Makes 2 cups. Each 1/4-cup serving: 70 calories; 234 mg sodium; 0 mg cholesterol; 4.4 g fat; 5.5 g carbohydrate; 1.9 g protein; 1.3 g fiber.

MAIN
COURSES

Dr. William D. Stimack and Barbara Rolek

SQUASH ITALIANO

Vegetables and protein with great fall colors.

2 medium butternut squash, about 2 pounds
2 Boca Italian sausages,* thawed and diced
2 teaspoons olive oil
1 small yellow onion, small dice
1/2 red pepper, small dice
1/2 green pepper, small dice
1 organic egg
1 cup multi-grain bread crumbs
1/2 to 1 cup steam-distilled water

- Preheat oven to 350 F. Wash squash, halve lengthwise and seed. Place cut side up in roasting pan. If necessary, remove a thin strip of skin from underside so squash will not rock. Meanwhile, heat oil in sauté pan and cook onion and peppers until almost tender. Remove from heat and mix with diced sausage, egg and bread crumbs.
- Fill each squash with 1/4 of the mixture. Place in a baking pan with 1/2 to 1 cup water. Bake for 45 minutes to 1 hour or until tender, covering with parchment paper if filling becomes too brown.

Makes 4 servings. Each serving: 157 calories; 617 mg sodium; 0 mg cholesterol; 3.3 g fat; 25.4 g carbohydrate; 6.1 g protein; 4.7 g fiber.

Dr. William D. Stimack and Barbara Rolek

MIDDLE EASTERN STEW

*Add a crunchy, cabbage-based salad
and warm whole-wheat bread for a hearty meal.*

1 tablespoon olive oil
2 large onions, chopped
2 medium potatoes, scrubbed and cut into 1/2-inch
    chunks
2 heaping cups peeled butternut squash, cut into 1/2-inch
    chunks
2 large carrots, peeled and cut into 1/2-inch dice
16 ounces tomatoes, diced
2 teaspoons ground cumin
1 teaspoon ground turmeric
10 ounces cooked chickpeas or 1 (15-ounce) can, drained
1 cup whole-wheat couscous*
1/4 cup chopped fresh flat-leaf parsley
3 to 4 green onions (white and light green parts), chopped

- In soup pot, heat oil over medium heat. Add onions and cook, stirring until softened, about 5 minutes. Add potatoes, squash, carrots, tomatoes and barely enough water to cover. Bring to a simmer, then add cumin and turmeric. Simmer gently, covered, until vegetables are tender, about 25 minutes. Add chickpeas and season to taste with salt and pepper. Simmer over low heat another 5 minutes.
- Meanwhile, put couscous into an ovenproof bowl and cover with 2 cups boiling water. Cover bowl and let stand 5 to 10 minutes, then fluff with fork. Place small amount of

couscous in each of 6 serving bowls, then ladle some stew over and sprinkle with parsley and green onions.

Makes 6 servings. Each serving: 301 calories; 82 mg sodium; 0 mg cholesterol; 5 g fat; 51 g carbohydrate; 9 g protein; 5 g fiber.

FAJITAS WITH AVOCADO "SOUR CREAM" SAUCE

Serve with shredded romaine lettuce topped with salsa.

1/2 pound seitan,* cut into 1/2-inch pieces
3 teaspoons olive oil, separated
2 medium onions, thinly sliced
3 cloves garlic, minced
2 medium red bell peppers, cut into 1-inch squares
1/2 teaspoon dried oregano
3/4 cup vegetable stock†
4 green onions (white and light green parts), cut into 1-inch pieces
1 ripe medium avocado, chopped
8 ounces soy sour cream*
1 jalapeño pepper, seeds removed
1 tablespoon fresh lime juice
3/4 teaspoon non-iodized sea salt
1/4 cup chopped cilantro
4 whole-wheat tortillas*

- Heat 2 teaspoons oil over medium heat in large skillet. Add seitan and cook, stirring occasionally, until browned, about 6 minutes. Remove from pan and set aside.
- Heat remaining teaspoon oil over medium heat in same skillet. Add onions and cook, stirring often, until they begin to caramelize, 5 to 6 minutes. Add garlic, red pepper and oregano and cook, stirring often, about 5 minutes. Stir in stock and reserved seitan and simmer until red pepper is

tender, 3 minutes. Add green onions and salt and black pepper to taste. Stir 1 to 2 minutes more.

- In food processor, make sauce by combining avocado, soy sour cream, jalapeño, lime juice and 3/4 teaspoon salt. Process until smooth and creamy. Add cilantro and pulse to combine. Adjust seasonings if necessary.
- Warm tortillas briefly in heated skillet. Serve tortillas mounded with seitan mixture and a generous dollop of avocado "sour cream" sauce.

Makes 4 servings. Each serving: 386 calories; 822 mg sodium; 1 mg cholesterol; 10 g fat; 50 g carbohydrate; 23 g protein; 9 g fiber.

Dr. William D. Stimack and Barbara Rolek

MUSHROOM STROGANOFF

*All the flavor of the original
without the meat!*

1 pound whole-wheat noodles
2 tablespoons olive oil
1 medium onion, finely chopped
1 garlic clove, minced
16 ounces fresh mushrooms, sliced (shiitake, cremini and
    button work well)
1 1/2 teaspoons minced fresh thyme or 1/2 teaspoon dried
    thyme
3 tablespoons minced fresh dill or 1 tablespoon dried dill
3 tablespoons minced fresh parsley or 1 tablespoon dried
1/2 cup soy sour cream*

- Boil noodles according to package directions. Meanwhile, in a large skillet over medium heat, sauté onion and garlic in oil until tender, about 5 minutes. Add mushrooms and herbs and continue to sauté until the mushrooms are tender. Add soy sour cream, mixing well. Portion hot noodles onto plates and top with mushroom stroganoff. Garnish with parsley if desired.

Makes 4 servings. Each serving: 157 calories; 617 mg sodium; 0 mg cholesterol; 3.3 g fat; 25.4 g carbohydrate; 6.1 g protein; 4.7 g fiber.

EGGPLANT PARMESAN

As tempting and flavorful as the original
without all the guilt.

1 large eggplant (about 2 pounds)
2 tablespoons vegetable stock†
1 medium onion, chopped
3 large cloves garlic, minced
1 medium green bell pepper, chopped
4 cups peeled and chopped tomatoes
1 tablespoon chopped fresh basil or 1 teaspoon dried
1 tablespoon chopped fresh flat-leaf parsley
1 teaspoon chopped fresh thyme or 1/4 teaspoon dried
1/4 to 1/3 cup steam-distilled water or vegetable stock†
1/2 to 1 cup dry bread crumbs
3/4 cup mozzarella-flavored soy cheese
1/4 to 1/2 cup grated parmesan-flavored soy topping

- Peel eggplant, then cut crosswise into 1/2-inch slices. Layer in colander, lightly sprinkling sea salt between layers. Place a 2- to 3-pound weight, such as a pot of water or large can of tomatoes, on top. Leave on 30 minutes or longer while eggplant drains, then rinse and pat dry.
- Meanwhile, in large, heavy-bottomed pot, heat stock over medium heat. Add onion and cook, stirring often, until softened, about 5 minutes. Add garlic and bell pepper and cook, stirring often, until vegetables are tender, about 7 minutes. Season to taste with black pepper. Add tomatoes, cover and cook over low heat 10 minutes. Uncover pot, stir

in 1/2 teaspoon sea salt and simmer gently until sauce thickens, about 1 hour. Add herbs and simmer 2 minutes longer. Taste and add more sea salt if necessary. Remove from heat.

- Preheat oven to 350 F. Coat large baking sheet with canola oil. Dip eggplant slices in water or stock, then in bread crumbs until well coated, and arrange on prepared sheet. Bake until eggplant is tender and crumbs are crisp, about 30 minutes.
- Spread a thin layer of sauce on the bottom of an 8" baking dish and arrange half the eggplant slices on top. Scatter 1/3 of the mozzarella on top, a layer of sauce and parmesan. Repeat, beginning with eggplant and ending with parmesan.
- Cover and bake until heated through, about 30 minutes. Uncover, sprinkle on remaining mozzarella and bake until cheese is melted and bubbly, about 10 minutes. Remove from oven, let stand a few minutes and serve hot.

Makes 6 servings. Each serving: 225 calories; 608 mg sodium; 17 mg cholesterol; 7 g fat; 28 g carbohydrate; 13 g protein; 5 g fiber.

RED PEPPER TOFU FRITTATA

Just add a green salad and fresh fruit
for a complete meal morning, noon or night!

1 tablespoon olive oil
1 large red bell pepper, diced
6 organic eggs
1/2 cup grated parmesan-flavored soy cheese
7 ounces firm or extra-firm tofu, drained and crumbled
1/3 cup chopped green onions, green part only
1/4 cup thinly sliced fresh basil leaves
1/4 teaspoon non-iodized sea salt
1/3 teaspoon pepper

- Heat oil in skillet over medium heat. Add red pepper and sauté until softened but not browned, about 4 minutes. Drain away any excess liquid; set aside.
- Whisk eggs and cheese in medium bowl. Stir in red pepper, tofu, green onions, basil, salt and pepper. Pour egg mixture into skillet and cook, without stirring, over medium heat, until bottom is set, about 4 minutes.
- Wrap skillet handle with foil. Broil frittata until top is light brown and no longer runny, about 2 minutes. Loosen bottom with rubber spatula and slide onto serving plate. Cut into wedges and serve hot or at room temperature.

Makes 4 servings. Each serving: 276 calories; 475 mg sodium; 328 mg cholesterol; 19 g fat; 5 g carbohydrate; 23 g protein; 0.22 g fiber.

Dr. William D. Stimack and Barbara Rolek

SEITAN SAUTÉ OVER SOBA NOODLES

Seitan, a wheat-gluten meat alternative, mixed with low-fat Oriental buckwheat noodles.

1 (8-ounce) package of soba noodles
1 bunch green onions including tops, cut into 1/2" pieces
5 to 6 fresh large button mushrooms, thinly sliced
10 cloves of garlic, minced
1 cup seitan,* chopped
1 tablespoon yellow miso
1/4 to 1/2 cup steam-distilled water

- In a medium frying pan, cook all ingredients except the noodles in the water, adding more as you need it.
- Meanwhile, cook the soba noodles according to package directions.
- When the mushrooms are cooked, turn off heat, and serve over drained and rinsed soba noodles.

Makes 4 servings. Each serving: 215 calories; 348 mg sodium; 0 mg cholesterol; 2.2 g fat; 36.6 g carbohydrate; 12.1 g protein; 6.4 g fiber.

TOFU STIR-FRY MEDLEY

This colorful dish is perfect for company.

1 pound firm tofu, drained and pressed (see "Before You
    Start Cooking")
1 tablespoon canola oil for frying
3 tablespoons light sesame oil
1 teaspoon garlic, minced
2 tablespoons fresh gingerroot, grated
4 ounces broccoli florets
4 ounces pea pods
1/2 cup red pepper, julienned
1/2 cup yellow pepper, julienned
1/2 cup leeks, julienned
2 ounces unsalted dry-roasted peanuts
1 cup mushrooms, sliced
1 cup pineapple juice
1/4 cup tamari*
1 tablespoon spelt flour*
8 ounces fresh pineapple, diced small
1/2 cup fresh orange sections, cut in half

- Cut tofu into cubes and fry in hot canola oil until golden. Drain and reserve. Wipe skillet clean and heat sesame oil in it. Sauté garlic and ginger until lightly browned. Add next 7 ingredients in order given. Stir-fry until vegetables are crisp-tender.
- In a bowl, combine juice, tamari and flour until smooth. Stir into pan, thoroughly coating ingredients. Cook for a few

minutes and toss in diced pineapple, orange sections and tofu. Mix well. Serve hot over brown rice, if desired.

Makes 6 servings. Each serving: 281 calories; 705 mg sodium; 0 mg cholesterol; 16.1 g fat; 23.6 g carbohydrate; 10.8 g protein; 3.9 g fiber.

FISH
AND
SEAFOOD

Dr. William D. Stimack and Barbara Rolek

TUNA WITH CITRUS SALAD

A refreshing, easy meal with a built-in
spicy citrus salad.

1/2 teaspoon arrowroot*
1/2 cup fish or vegetable stock†
1 medium pink grapefruit
1 medium orange
1 tablespoon minced jalapeño pepper
1 tablespoon peanut oil
Freshly ground black pepper
1/4 teaspoon non-iodized sea salt
1 pound trimmed yellowfin or ahi tuna fillet, cut into 4
    pieces
1/2 teaspoon finely grated lemon zest
1/2 teaspoon finely grated lime zest
1 cup very thinly sliced fennel bulb
1 red onion, very thinly sliced
2 teaspoons chopped fennel tops

- In small bowl, dissolve arrowroot in 2 teaspoons stock. Bring remaining stock to boil in small saucepan. Add arrowroot mixture and cook, stirring until thickened, about 30 seconds. Remove from heat and let cool slightly.
- Remove rind from grapefruit and orange. Separate into sections, removing all membrane. Work over a bowl to catch the juices. Add jalapeño and citrus juice to thickened stock. Whisk in oil and season with pepper.

151

- Brush broiler rack with oil and set under medium-high heat. Season tuna with salt and pepper. Broil 5" from heat until opaque in center, 2 to 3 minutes per side.
- Meanwhile, warm dressing. Add grapefruit and orange sections and lemon and lime zest; warm through. Divide and arrange fennel on each of four plates and top with onion. Arrange citrus salad next to fennel. Drizzle plates with dressing and sprinkle with chopped fennel tops.

Makes 4 servings. Each serving: 244 calories; 273 mg sodium; 43 mg cholesterol; 9 g fat; 12 g carbohydrate; 28 g protein; 3 g fiber.

SEA BASS IN TOMATO SAUCE

2 1/2 pounds sea bass, tuna or salmon fillets
2 onions, sliced in rings
2 carrots, thinly sliced and steamed tender-crisp
1 small green pepper, chopped
2 garlic cloves, minced
Juice of 2 lemons (5 tablespoons)
1 cup vegetable or fish stock†
1 cup tomato sauce†
1/4 cup chopped parsley
12 small green olives, sliced in half

- Preheat oven to 350 F. Place fish in glass baking dish and arrange onions, carrots, green pepper and garlic around the fish. Combine lemon juice, stock and tomato sauce and pour over fish. Bake uncovered for 20 minutes. Add parsley and olives. Continue to bake uncovered for another 15 to 20 minutes or until the fish is opaque and flakes easily.

Makers 6 servings. Each serving: 256 calories; 429 mg sodium; 18 mg cholesterol; 4.6 g fat; 17 g carbohydrate; 37.1 g protein; 3.9 g fiber.

Dr. William D. Stimack and Barbara Rolek

"PARMESAN" BAKED COD

4 (6-ounce) pieces Alaskan cod fillets
1/2 cup organic unbleached white or spelt flour*
1/2 cup stone-ground corn meal
1/2 teaspoon non-iodized sea salt
1/4 teaspoon onion powder
1/4 teaspoon freshly ground black pepper
2 tablespoons olive oil
1/2 cup parmesan-flavored soy topping

- Preheat oven to 450 F. Rinse and drain fillets. Combine flour, corn meal and seasonings. Pour oil into bottom of an 8" glass baking dish. Dredge cod in flour mixture and place in pan. Turn to coat with oil. Sprinkle tops of cod with parmesan. Bake for 8 to 10 minutes or until fish flakes easily with a fork.

Makes 4 servings. Each serving: 312 calories; 692 mg sodium; 73 mg cholesterol; 9.1 g fat; 22.9 g carbohydrate; 34.6 g protein; 2.9 g fiber.

POACHED SALMON WITH ASPARAGUS-RICE PILAF

Poaching is an easy, low-fat way to cook fish.

2 lemons
1 quart fish or vegetable stock†
2 tablespoons olive oil
2 large shallots, minced
1 1/2 cups basmati rice*
Freshly ground black pepper, to taste
1 pound asparagus, tough ends removed, cut into 1"
    pieces
2 tablespoons rice vinegar
1 bay leaf
4 (8-ounce) salmon fillets
2 green onions, chopped

- Remove zest from one lemon; mince. Set aside. Juice two lemons into measuring cup. Heat stock in large pot. Meanwhile, heat oil in Dutch oven; add shallots and cook until tender, about 2 minutes. Stir in rice and coat grains with oil. Add 2 1/2 cups heated stock, 1/4 cup lemon juice and few grindings of pepper. Heat to boiling; reduce to simmer. Cover; cook 10 minutes.

- Stir lemon zest and asparagus into rice. Return to simmer; cover. Cook until rice is tender, about 10 minutes. Let stand, covered, a few minutes before serving.

- Meanwhile, in a large, shallow pan, add 4 cups water to remaining stock; heat to simmering. Stir remaining lemon juice into heated stock; add vinegar and bay leaf. Heat to boiling. Add salmon; reduce heat and poach until flaky but still pink in center of thickest part, 5 to 6 minutes. If fillets are not completely covered by liquid, cover pan. Carefully lift fillets from broth. Serve over rice pilaf garnished with green onions.

Makes 4 servings. Each serving: 750 calories; 465 mg sodium; 135 mg cholesterol; 27 g fat; 70 g carbohydrate; 57 g protein; 3 g fiber.

BROILED SWORDFISH WITH MANGO SALSA

This salsa is great with any fish and it's even terrific with tortilla chips.

Salsa:

1 cup diced firm-ripe mango
1/4 pound Roma tomatoes, cored and coarsely chopped
1/2 cup each orange and yellow bell peppers
1/4 cup finely diced red onion
1 tablespoon minced fresh jalapeño chile
1 tablespoon chopped fresh cilantro
1 clove garlic, peeled and minced
2 tablespoons lime juice
1 tablespoon rice vinegar
non-iodized sea salt and freshly ground black pepper to taste

- In a medium bowl, combine all ingredients. Serve or cover and chill up to 1 day to let the flavors marry.

Makes 4 cups. Each 1/4 cup: 26 calories; 44 mg sodium; 0 mg cholesterol; 0.2 g fat; 5 g carbohydrate; 1 g protein; 1 g fiber.

Swordfish:

1/4 cup canola oil

1/4 cup lime juice
3 jalapeños, seeded and chopped
1 teaspoon minced garlic
1/4 cup chopped cilantro
1 teaspoon freshly ground black pepper
1/4 cup freshly grated gingerroot
1/4 cup soy or rice milk
4 (6-ounce) swordfish steaks

- Combine first 8 ingredients in the bowl of a food processor fitted with a metal blade and pulse to combine. Rinse swordfish and pat dry. Rub steaks with marinade, cover and marinate, refrigerated, overnight. Broil until fish is well colored on both sides and the interior is medium (about 5 minutes total). Serve with mango salsa.

Makes 4 servings. Each serving without salsa: 356 calories; 161 mg sodium; 66 mg cholesterol; 21.6 g fat; 4.4 g carbohydrate; 35.8 g protein; 1.4 g fiber.

SALMON AND NEW POTATO SALAD

Chunks of salmon and steamed new potatoes
dressed with vinaigrette and tossed with onions.

1 pound small new potatoes
3/4 pound salmon fillet
1/2 cup fish or vegetable stock†
1 bay leaf
3/4 cup extra-virgin olive oil
4 tablespoons red-wine vinegar
1 clove garlic, smashed
1 teaspoon Dijon mustard
Non-iodized sea salt and freshly ground black pepper
2 tablespoons chopped fresh mint
1 tablespoon capers, drained
6 romaine lettuce leaves

- Steam or boil potatoes until tender, about 15 minutes. Drain; cool slightly. Meanwhile, place salmon in saucepan; add stock and bay leaf and enough cold water to barely cover fish. Heat till water barely trembles. Simmer slowly 20 minutes. Remove fish from poaching liquid; cool.
- Combine oil, vinegar, garlic and mustard in lidded jar. Shake well. Season with salt and pepper. Cut each potato in half while still warm; place in large bowl. Break fish into bite-size chunks; add to potatoes. Add mint and capers. Drizzle oil mixture over all; toss gently. Add more salt if desired. Chill or cool to room temperature.

- Place 2 lettuce leaves on each of 3 plates. Mound salad on lettuce and serve.

Makes 3 servings.   Each serving: 750 calories; 210 mg sodium; 65 mg cholesterol; 63 g fat; 21 g carbohydrate; 26 g protein; 3 g fiber.

CHUNKY GUACAMOLE AND SHRIMP

*This makes a great appetizer or a filling
main-course with the addition of soup.*

1 ripe avocado, halved, pit removed
1 tablespoon Nayonaise*
2 teaspoons minced onion
2 teaspoons fresh lime juice
1/2 jalapeño, seeded and minced
Non-iodized sea salt
Freshly ground black pepper
4 (7-inch) whole-wheat tortillas*
1/2 cup loosely packed cilantro
12 cooked medium shrimp, split lengthwise, veins
   removed
8 large, firm cherry tomatoes, sliced paper thin
Cilantro sprigs, for garnish

- Coarsely mash avocado in bowl with a fork. Stir in Nayonaise, onion, lime juice and jalapeño, then salt and pepper to taste.
- Spread avocado mixture on tortillas to the edges, about 2 tablespoons on each. Scatter about 12 cilantro leaves on each. Place 6 shrimp halves across the top 1/4 of the tortilla. Place tomatoes over shrimp, dividing evenly. Start with shrimp end and roll up tightly. Wrap airtight in plastic, twist ends closed. Refrigerate 2 to 6 hours.

- Cut each in half and place on a plate with a soup accompaniment. Or cut each in four pieces and arrange on a platter to serve as appetizers.

Makes 4 servings. Each serving: 320 calories; 600 mg sodium; 300 mg cholesterol; 8 g fat; 22 g carbohydrate; 40 g protein; 3 g fiber.

POTATO-CRUSTED SALMON
WITH CUCUMBER SAUCE

*The low-fat cucumber sauce adds a fresh accent
to this fish.*

1/2 cup soy sour cream*
1/4 cup chopped seeded cucumbers
1/2 teaspoon dried dill weed
4 (4-ounce) skinless salmon fillets
1/4 teaspoon non-iodized sea salt
1/4 teaspoon freshly ground black pepper
2 cups shredded fresh potatoes
1 tablespoon olive oil
Lemon wedges and kalamata olives, optional

- In small bowl, combine sour cream, cucumber and dill; set aside. Pat fish dry with paper towels and season with salt and pepper. Place 1/2 cup potato on top of each fillet, pressing firmly to form an even layer.
- In large skillet, heat oil over medium heat until hot. Place fillets, potato side down in skillet. Cook 8 to 10 minutes without turning until potatoes are golden brown. Using large spatula, carefully turn fillets over; cook an additional 4 to 6 minutes or until fish is cooked to desired doneness. Serve warm with sauce and lemon and olives, if desired.

Makes 4 servings. Each serving: 362 calories; 351 mg sodium; 75 mg cholesterol; 18 g fat; 21 g carbohydrate; 27 g protein; 2 g fiber.

Dr. William D. Stimack and Barbara Rolek

WRAPS
AND
BURGERS

Dr. William D. Stimack and Barbara Rolek

TEMPEH WRAP WITH
THAI-STYLE "PEANUT" SAUCE

Delicious contrast between crusty tempeh
and the crunch of fresh salad greens.

2 tablespoons soynut butter*
1 tablespoon tamari*
1 tablespoon lime juice
1/4 teaspoon hot red pepper flakes
1/4 cup hot steam-distilled water
8 ounces tempeh,* cut into 1/2-inch squares
1 medium cucumber, peeled, seeded and diced
1 medium carrot, shredded
4 medium green onions, cut into 1/2-inch lengths
1/4 cup whole fresh cilantro leaves
1 tablespoon peanut oil
4 small romaine lettuce leaves, washed, dried and torn in
    half
4 large whole-wheat tortillas,* warmed

- Whisk soynut butter, tamari, lime juice, pepper flakes and hot water together in medium bowl. Transfer 3 tablespoons sauce to small bowl and reserve. Add tempeh to bowl with remaining sauce and marinate for 15 to 20 minutes, tossing occasionally.
- Place cucumber, carrot, green onions and cilantro in medium bowl; set aside. Heat oil in skillet over medium heat. Add tempeh and cook until golden brown all over, about 4 minutes. Remove skillet from heat.

- Pour reserved 3 tablespoons peanut sauce over cucumber salad and toss to combine. Place two pieces of lettuce on bottom half of each wrap. Spoon over some cucumber salad and top with several pieces of tempeh. Roll up, tucking sides toward center to form bundles. Slice each roll in half and serve.

Makes 4 servings. Each serving: 299 calories, 292 mg sodium; 13 g fat; 31 g carbohydrate; 17 g protein; 6 g fiber.

HARVEST VEGETABLE WRAPS

A ratatouille-like filling rolled in
tortillas with lightly dressed baby spinach.

2 tablespoons plus 1 teaspoon extra-virgin olive oil
1 medium onion, chopped
1 medium red bell pepper, cored, seeded and chopped
1 small eggplant, chopped (about 1 1/2 cups)
1 medium zucchini, chopped (about 1 1/2 cups)
2 medium garlic cloves, minced
Non-iodized sea salt and ground black pepper
1 tablespoon plus 1 teaspoon balsamic vinegar
2 tablespoons minced fresh basil
3 cups baby spinach leaves, washed and dried
4 large whole-wheat tortillas,* warmed

- Heat 2 tablespoons oil in large skillet. Add onion, bell pepper, eggplant and zucchini and cook over medium heat until lightly browned, about 7 minutes. Stir in garlic, season with salt and pepper to taste, and add 1 tablespoon vinegar. Cover and cook until vegetables are tender, about 5 minutes. Stir in basil and remove from heat; cool slightly.
- Place spinach in medium bowl. Drizzle with remaining 1 teaspoon vinegar and remaining 1 teaspoon oil. Sprinkle with salt and pepper to taste.
- Place some spinach on bottom half of each tortilla. Spoon some vegetables over and roll up, tucking sides toward center to form bundles. Slice each roll in half and serve immediately.

Makes 4 servings. Each serving: 192 calories; 413 mg sodium; 10 g fat; 23 g carbohydrate; 5 g protein; 4 g fiber.

TERIYAKI MUSHROOM WRAPS

Portabello mushrooms the Asian way!

4 medium portabello mushrooms, stems discarded
1/4 cup teriyaki sauce (see note below)
4 cups watercress or other baby greens, tough stems
    removed
1 teaspoon rice vinegar
1 teaspoon tamari
2 teaspoons sesame oil
4 large whole-wheat tortillas,* warmed

- Heat broiler. Brush mushrooms with teriyaki sauce and marinate for 10 minutes. Broil, turning once, until lightly browned, 8 to 10 minutes. Cut mushrooms in half and then into strips.
- Meanwhile, toss watercress, vinegar, tamari and sesame oil in medium bowl. Place some watercress on bottom half of each wrap.
- Arrange some mushroom strips over greens and roll up wraps, tucking sides toward center to form bundles. Slice each roll in half and serve immediately.

Note: To make your own teriyaki sauce, mix equal parts of tamari,* sake and mirin*.

Makes 4 servings. Each serving: 146 calories; 827 mg sodium; 4 g fat; 23 g carbohydrate; 6 g protein; 3 g fiber.

SOUTHWESTERN POTATO-CORN WRAPS

*Warm potato-corn salad pairs up with arugula to
make a delicious wrap filling.*

3/4 pound red potatoes, scrubbed and cut into 1/2-inch
    dice
Non-iodized sea salt
1 medium ear corn, husked and silked, kernels removed
    (about 3/4 cup)
1 small tomato, cored and diced
3 medium green onions, white and light green parts only,
    minced
1 tablespoon lime juice
2 tablespoons extra-virgin olive oil
3/4 teaspoon chili powder
1/4 teaspoon cayenne pepper, or to taste
2 cups stemmed arugula leaves, washed and dried
4 large whole-wheat tortillas,* warmed

- Place potatoes and water to cover in large saucepan. Bring
to boil, add salt to taste; reduce heat and cook briskly until
potatoes are almost tender, about 8 minutes. Stir in corn and
cook until potatoes and corn are tender, about 3 minutes
more.
- Drain potatoes and corn and transfer to large bowl. Add
tomato and green onions and stir to combine. Drizzle lime
juice and oil over vegetables and sprinkle with chili powder
and cayenne. Toss gently and add salt to taste.

- Place some arugula on the bottom half of each wrap. Spoon some potato-corn mixture over the greens and roll up wraps, tucking sides toward center to form bundles. Slice each roll in half and serve immediately.

Makes 4 servings. Each serving: 257 calories; 399 mg sodium; 9 g fat; 41 g carbohydrate; 6 g protein; 2 g fiber.

BLACK BEAN AND RICE BURRITO

2 (15-ounce cans) organic Southwestern style black
    beans, drained
2 cups cooked brown rice*
4 cups chopped tomatoes
1 cup chopped green pepper
1 cup chopped onion
3 cloves garlic, minced
1 jalapeño pepper, minced
1/4 teaspoon cayenne pepper
1 teaspoon cumin
1/4 teaspoon chili powder
1 cup grated soy cheese*
8 whole-wheat tortillas*

- Purée beans in food processor. Place in large bowl and mix with rice. Add tomatoes, green pepper, onion, garlic, jalapeño, cayenne, cumin and chili powder. Adjust seasoning if necessary. Place a line of bean mixture down center of warm tortilla. Add cheese, fold over ends and roll.

Makes 8 servings. Each serving: 275 calories; 313 mg sodium; 0 mg cholesterol; 2.5 g fat; 50.4 g carbohydrate; 12.9 g protein; 10.9 g fiber.

VEGGIE BEAN BURGERS

A meatless version of everyone's
favorite—hamburgers!

1/2 cup soy sour cream*
2 tablespoons green onions, chopped
Pinch of dried oregano
1 (15-ounce) can organic kidney beans, drained and
  rinsed
3 tablespoons dried whole-grain bread crumbs
1/4 teaspoon garlic powder
Dash of black pepper
1 organic egg, beaten
2 teaspoons canola oil for frying

- In a small bowl, combine soy sour cream, onions and oregano. Chill until serving time.
- In a medium bowl, mash beans with fork. Add bread crumbs, garlic powder, pepper and egg. Mix well. Shape into 4 patties. Add oil to skillet and fry patties for 5 minutes on each side. Top each with a dollop of soy sour cream.

Makes 4 servings. Each serving: 156 calories; 215 mg sodium; 24 mg cholesterol; 25 g carbohydrate; 10 g protein.

MUSHROOM-BARLEY BURGERS

*With their delicate herbed flavor, these are
sure to be a hit at your next barbecue!*

1 1/2 cups uncooked barley
3 cups steam-distilled water
1 1/2 cups steam-distilled water
1 cup old-fashioned rolled oats*
2 garlic cloves, peeled and pressed
1 teaspoon garlic powder
1 medium onion, peeled and finely chopped
1 large rib celery, minced
1 teaspoon each marjoram and basil, OR Italian
   seasoning OR dill
2 teaspoons olive oil
1 pound mushrooms, coarsely chopped
1/4 cup sesame tahini*
1/4 cup sunflower seeds
1 1/2 tablespoons tamari*

- Cook barley in 3 cups water and set aside. Meanwhile, boil 1 1/2 cups water, then add oats. Leave covered, turn off heat and set aside.
- In a skillet, sauté garlic, garlic powder, onion, celery and herbs in olive oil until onion is slightly translucent. Add chopped mushrooms and continue cooking until most of the liquid has evaporated.
- In a bowl, combine together all remaining ingredients until evenly blended. Form into eight 3" burgers. Lightly coat

broiler rack with oil and broil burgers until brown on each side.

Makes 8 servings. Each serving: 316 calories; 208 mg sodium; 0 mg cholesterol; 9.5 g fat; 45.9 g carbohydrate; 11.7 g protein; 10.1 g fiber.

Dr. William D. Stimack and Barbara Rolek

GREEN GODDESS BURGERS

*Try this served in a whole-wheat pita topped
with additional slices of avocado and tomatoes.*

2 tablespoons sesame seeds
2 tablespoons sunflower seeds
1/2 cup old-fashioned rolled oats*
1/2 cup cooked short-grain brown rice*
1/2 cup cooked lentils
1/2 cup cooked beans, such as white navy beans
1/2 cup minced onions
1/2 cup fine dry whole-grain bread crumbs
2 tablespoons chopped pecans
1/4 cup chopped fresh parsley
1/2 teaspoon Italian herb seasoning or 1 teaspoon fresh
    herbs
1 tablespoon organic tomato purée
1 tablespoon sesame tahini*
1/3 cup chopped fresh mushrooms
1/2 sliced avocado, chopped
Additional avocado and tomato slices for garnish

- Process seeds and rolled oats in a blender until ground. Mix
  with remaining ingredients except garnish and shape into 8
  patties. Lightly coat broiler rack with oil and broil patties
  until browned on both sides.

Makes 8 servings. Each serving: 201 calories; 207 mg sodium; 0 mg cholesterol; 8.7 g fat; 24 g carbohydrate; 7 g protein; 4.9 g fiber.

SLOPPY JOE LENTILS

1 medium onion, chopped
1 clove garlic, minced
1 tablespoon canola or olive oil
1 whole carrot, chopped
3 tablespoons fresh chopped parsley
1/2 teaspoon dried basil
1 tablespoon tamari*
4 cups vegetable stock†
2 cups lentils, uncooked
3 cups tomato sauce† or barbecue sauce†
Whole-wheat buns or brown rice*

- Sauté onion and garlic in oil until translucent. Add carrots and herbs; cook 5 minutes. Add tamari, stock and lentils; simmer 30 minutes. Add tomato sauce or barbecue sauce and simmer until vegetables and lentils are tender. Add water if too thick. Serve on buns or over rice.

Makes 6 servings. Each serving without the bun or rice: 306 calories; 335 mg sodium; 0 mg cholesterol; 5.2 g fat; 47.2 g carbohydrate; 17.7 g protein; 9 g fiber.

PIZZAS

Dr. William D. Stimack and Barbara Rolek

PUSH-BUTTON PIZZA DOUGH

3/4 cup warm steam-distilled water (105 F. to 115 F.)
1 1/2 teaspoons active dry yeast
1/2 teaspoon non-iodized sea salt
2 teaspoons olive oil, plus more as needed
1/2 teaspoon turbinado sugar*
1 3/4 cups plus 1 tablespoon organic unbleached white
   flour

- Place warm water in food processor bowl. Sprinkle yeast over, then add salt, 2 teaspoons oil and sugar. Process briefly to mix. Let rest 1 minute. Add 1 3/4 cups flour and process in two 4-second bursts, waiting several seconds between each. Process one more 4-second burst, adding remaining 1 tablespoon flour with machine running. Let dough rest 1 minute.
- Lightly oil medium bowl. Turn dough out only lightly floured surface (it will be somewhat sticky). With floured hands, knead gently 30 to 45 seconds. Place dough in oiled bowl, rotating to coat entire surface. Cover with plastic wrap and set aside in warm spot to rise until doubled in bulk, 1 to 1 1/2 hours. Proceed as directed in individual recipes.

Makes 2 small or 1 large pizza. Per 1/8 of dough: 112 calories; 388 mg sodium; 0 mg cholesterol; 1 g fat; 21 g carbohydrate; 3 g protein; 1 g fiber.

SPELT PIZZA DOUGH

1 package active dry yeast
1 cup warm steam-distilled water (105 F. to 115 F.)
3 cups whole spelt flour*
1/2 teaspoon non-iodized sea salt*

- In a small bowl, mix yeast in warm water. Stir and set aside for 5 to 10 minutes. In large bowl, combine flour and salt, mixing well. Add yeast mixture and stir thoroughly. Knead dough on well-floured surface 100 times or until soft, springy and no longer sticky. Return dough to bowl. Cover with damp towel and set in warm place to rise, about 1 hour or until doubled.
- Remove dough and knead on floured surface for 2 minutes. Proceed as directed in individual recipes.

Makes 2 small or 1 large pizza. Per 1/8 of dough: 166 calories; 149 mg sodium; 0 mg cholesterol; 0.8 g fat; 33 g carbohydrate; 6.5 g protein; 5.7 g fiber.

VEGGIE PIZZA

Good for you snack or main course.

1 large homemade crust†
1 teaspoon olive oil
2 ounces fresh mushrooms, sliced
1 small onion, sliced
1/2 zucchini, thinly sliced
1/2 green pepper, julienned
1 clove of garlic, minced
1 teaspoon fresh oregano, chopped
1 teaspoon fresh basil, chopped
3/4 cup organic pizza sauce or tomato sauce†
2 tablespoons parmesan-flavored soy topping*
1 medium tomato, thinly sliced
6 black olives, sliced into rings
8 ounces mozzarella-flavored soy cheese*

- Preheat oven to 350 F. In a skillet, lightly sauté mushrooms, onion, zucchini, green pepper, garlic, oregano and basil in oil. Remove from heat.
- Place pizza crust on a baking sheet. Spread crust with pizza sauce, then sprinkle with parmesan topping. Next spread on sautéed vegetables, sliced tomatoes, black olives and mozzarella shreds. Bake for approximately 15 minutes or until the cheese melts.

Makes 8 slices. Each slice using spelt pizza crust: 226 calories; 557 mg sodium; 1 mg cholesterol; 3.3 g fat; 39.2 g carbohydrate; 9.8 g protein; 7.2 g fiber.

TOMATO-PESTO PIZZA

Roasted tomatoes give this pizza
a concentrated flavor without the excess moisture.

1 batch pizza dough†
Olive oil
4 large ripe tomatoes, cut into 1/4" slices
Non-iodized sea salt and freshly ground black pepper
1/2 cup pesto sauce†
4 ounces mozzarella-flavored soy cheese*
1 tablespoon chopped fresh parsley

- Preheat oven to 350 F. Place tomato slices on parchment-lined rimmed baking sheet. Sprinkle with salt and pepper to taste. Roast until softened, about 25 minutes. Transfer pan to wire rack to cool; set aside.
- Turn oven temperature up to 450 F. Divide dough in half and roll each into a 9" circle, 1/4" thick. Transfer to two oiled baking pans. Lightly brush surface with oil, cover with plastic wrap and let rest 10 minutes.
- Spread pesto over crusts, top with tomato slices and sprinkle with cheese. Bake 15 to 20 minutes or until crust is brown and cheese is bubbly. Transfer to cutting board, sprinkle with parsley, slice and serve.

Makes 2 small pizzas (8 slices). Each serving: 222 calories; 671 mg sodium; 10 mg cholesterol; 10 g fat; 25 g carbohydrate; 7 g protein; 2 g fiber.

Dr. William D. Stimack and Barbara Rolek

"SAUSAGE" PIZZA

*Meaty portabello mushrooms take the place
of sausage in this tasty pizza.*

For sausage:

3 cups chopped portabello mushrooms
2 tablespoons olive oil
3 garlic cloves, minced
2 teaspoons fennel seed
1 1/2 teaspoons dried Italian herbs
3/4 teaspoon crushed red pepper
Non-iodized sea salt and freshly ground black pepper to
   taste

For pizza:

1 batch pizza dough†
8 ounces tomato sauce†
1 1/2 cups chopped green pepper
1 1/2 cups chopped red onion
3/4 cup mozzarella-flavored soy cheese

• Preheat oven to 450 F. Combine all sausage ingredients.
Divide dough in half and roll each into a 9" circle, 1/4"
thick. Transfer to two oiled baking pans. Lightly brush
surface with oil, cover with plastic wrap and let rest 10
minutes.

- Spread crusts with sauce, "sausage," pepper, onion and cheese. Bake for 10 to 12 minutes or until crust is golden and cheese is bubbly. Transfer to cutting board, slice and serve.

Makes 2 small pizzas (8 slices). Each serving: 329 calories; 482 mg sodium; 11 g fat; 45 g carbohydrate; 14 g protein; 4 g fiber.

Dr. William D. Stimack and Barbara Rolek

STARCHES

Dr. William D. Stimack and Barbara Rolek

LATIN ROASTED POTATOES

A low-fat version with a Mexican twist!

1 tablespoon olive oil
1 tablespoon chili powder
2 teaspoons finely chopped garlic
1/8 teaspoon non-iodized sea salt
1/2 teaspoon freshly ground black pepper
1 1/2 pounds (4 medium) potatoes
1 medium onion, cut into 1/2" thick wedges
1 1/2 cups halved cherry tomatoes
1/3 cup coarsely chopped fresh cilantro
1 tablespoon fresh lime juice
4 lime wedges, optional garnish

- Preheat oven to 425 F. On parchment-lined baking sheet, combine oil, chili powder, garlic, salt and pepper. Scrub potatoes; leave skin on; cut lengthwise into 1/2" thick wedges. Add them to pan with onion and toss to coat evenly. Bake 25 minutes. Add tomatoes; bake an additional 7 to 10 minutes or until potatoes are tender.
- Transfer to large bowl; add cilantro. Sprinkle with lime juice and toss lightly. Serve with lime wedges, if desired.

Makes 4 servings. Each serving: 280 calories; 80 mg sodium; 0 mg cholesterol; 5 g fat; 52 g carbohydrate; 5 g protein; 6 g fiber.

Dr. William D. Stimack and Barbara Rolek

ROASTED SWEET POTATO WEDGES

Instead of candied sweets, try these on for size!

1 medium-large sweet potato, peeled
1 tablespoon olive oil
1/8 teaspoon non-iodized sea salt
Freshly ground black pepper

- Preheat oven to 425 F. Cut potato in half lengthwise, then cut each half into 7 long, thin wedges. Place them on a rimmed baking sheet covered with parchment paper. Toss them with the oil, salt and pepper to taste, so all sides are coated.
- Bake 10 minutes. Flip potatoes over and bake another 8 to 10 minutes or until tender. Serve hot.

Makes 2 servings. Each serving: 126 calories; 152 mg sodium; 0 mg cholesterol; 7 g fat; 16 g carbohydrate; 1 g protein; 2.25 g fiber.

HERBED BROWN RICE PILAF

The nutty flavor of brown rice with garlic and herbs.

1 tablespoon olive oil
1 cup chopped onion
1 tablespoon finely chopped garlic
12 ounces short-grain brown rice*
2 cups hot vegetable stock†
2 tablespoons each chopped fresh basil, chives and
  parsley
3/4 teaspoon freshly ground black pepper
1/4 teaspoon non-iodized sea salt

- In 3-quart saucepan over medium heat, sauté onion and garlic in heated oil 2 to 3 minutes, stirring frequently until softened. Add brown rice; cook and stir 2 minutes.
- Add hot stock (stand back so the steam doesn't burn you), stir and reduce heat to low. Cook covered 30 to 40 minutes until rice is tender. Remove from heat. Stir in herbs, pepper and salt.

Makes 6 servings. Each serving: 261 calories; 322 mg sodium; 1 mg cholesterol; 5 g fat; 50 g carbohydrate; 6 g protein; 3 g fiber.

CAJUN BEANS AND BARLEY

*This side dish becomes a complete meal
with the addition of a green, leafy salad.*

1 1/2 cups steam-distilled water
1/2 cup barley
1/4 cup chopped green pepper
1/4 cup chopped onion
1 (15-ounce) can organic pinto beans, rinsed and drained
1 (14.5-ounce) can organic stewed tomatoes
1 cup frozen whole-kernel corn
1 teaspoon Cajun seasoning or 1/2 teaspoon crushed
    dried red pepper

- In medium saucepan, bring water to boiling. Stir in barley, green pepper and onion. Return to boil; reduce heat, cover and simmer 25 to 35 minutes or till barley is tender and water is absorbed.
- Stir in beans, tomatoes, corn and seasoning. Cook, covered, over medium heat till bubbly. Cook 2 to 3 minutes more or till corn is tender.

Makes 4 servings. Each serving: 240 calories; 610 mg sodium; 0 mg cholesterol; 1 g fat; 51 g carbohydrate; 10 g protein; 3 g fiber.

LENTILS AND GRAINS PILAF

A low-fat union of grains and legumes.

1 tablespoon olive oil
1/2 teaspoon non-iodized sea salt
1/3 cup short-grain brown rice*
1/3 cup wheat berries*
1/2 cup chopped onion
1/4 teaspoon dried savory, crushed
1/3 cup lentils
2 tablespoons snipped dried apricots or raisins
Freshly ground black pepper

- In medium saucepan, combine oil, salt and 1 cup water. Stir in rice, wheat berries, onion and savory. Bring to boil, reduce heat, cover and simmer for 20 minutes.
- Stir in lentils, return to a boil and reduce heat. Cover and simmer for 30 minutes more or till rice, lentils and wheat berries are tender. Drain off any excess liquid. Stir in apricots or raisins. Season to taste with pepper.

Makes 4 servings. Each serving: 165 calories; 262 mg sodium; 0 mg cholesterol; 3 g fat; 29 g carbohydrate; 6 g protein; 2 g fiber.

Dr. William D. Stimack and Barbara Rolek

COUSCOUS WITH DATES

Middle Eastern pasta with dates, raisins, ginger and cashews.

1 pound couscous*
Grated rind and juice from 1 orange
2 tablespoons extra-virgin olive oil
2 tablespoons apple cider vinegar
1/2 teaspoon turbinado sugar*
1/4 teaspoon non-iodized sea salt
3 ounces pitted dates
3 tablespoons chopped parsley
1 cup dark or light raisins
2 tablespoons crystallized ginger, coarsely chopped
6 ounces cashews

- Prepare couscous according to package directions, omitting butter and using vegetable stock instead of water.
- Cut each date into 3 pieces. In large bowl, mix orange peel and juice, oil, vinegar, sugar and salt. Add couscous, dates, parsley, raisins, ginger and cashews. Toss well. Serve hot or cold.

Makes 8 servings. Each serving: 481 calories; 248 mg sodium; 0 mg cholesterol; 14.1 g fat; 77.2 g carbohydrate; 11.6 g protein; 5.3 g fiber.

CONFETTI RICE

An explosion of rice, peppers, corn, peas,
pineapple and green onion.

1 pound short-grain brown rice*
8 ounces frozen corn, unthawed
8 ounces pineapple tidbits, drained
1 red pepper, diced small
1 green pepper, diced small
1 cup frozen peas, unthawed
4 green onions, chopped
1/2 cup chopped parsley
3/4 cup organic low-fat Italian dressing

- Prepare brown rice according to package directions. Drain if necessary. Mix with remaining ingredients. Serve hot or cold. If serving cold, rinse cooked rice under cold water before combining with remaining ingredients.

Makes 8 servings. Each serving: 390 calories; 202 mg sodium; 0 mg cholesterol; 12.7 g fat; 61.4 g carbohydrate; 7.2 g protein; 5.2 g fiber.

Dr. William D. Stimack and Barbara Rolek

WILD RICE

*A blend of dried cherries, almonds, raisins,
wild and brown rices.*

6-ounce box organic wild rice
1/2 cup short-grain brown rice*
1 cup chopped celery
1/2 cup chopped green onion
1/2 cup dark raisins
1/2 cup dried cherries
1/2 cup toasted slivered almonds
1/2 teaspoon non-iodized sea salt
2 tablespoons lemon juice
2 tablespoons balsamic vinegar

- Bring 2 3/4 cups water to a boil in medium saucepan. Add wild rice, cover and simmer until tender, about 45 minutes. Let stand 5 minutes until all water is absorbed. Fluff rice and spoon into a bowl.
- Meanwhile, bring 1 cup water to boil in small saucepan. Add brown rice, cover and cook until tender, about 15 to 20 minutes. Fluff rice and lightly stir into cooked wild rice.
- Stir celery, green onions, raisins, cherries, almonds and salt into rices. Drizzle over lemon juice and balsamic vinegar and toss well. Serve warm or cold.

Makes 10 servings. Each 1/2-cup serving: 86 calories; 130 mg sodium; 0 mg cholesterol; 4 grams fat; 3 grams protein; 1.78 grams fiber.

VEGETABLES

Dr. William D. Stimack and Barbara Rolek

ROASTED VEGETABLES

This high-temperature cooking technique
adds rich, robust flavor to vegetables.

2 tablespoons olive oil
1 teaspoon non-iodized sea salt
1/4 teaspoon dried marjoram leaves
1/4 teaspoon black pepper
4 medium russet potatoes, unpeeled, cut into 1 1/2"
    chunks
2 medium carrots, julienned
1 to 2 parsnips, julienned
1 red onion, cut into 8 wedges
1 medium green bell pepper, cut into 8 pieces
8 cloves garlic

- Preheat oven to 450 F. In large bowl, combine oil, salt, marjoram and pepper; mix well. Add all remaining ingredients; toss to coat. Spread on parchment-lined 15"x10"x1" baking pan.
- Bake for 20 minutes. Turn and stir vegetables. Bake an additional 20 to 25 minutes or until vegetables are tender, stirring once. Serve as an accompaniment to fish, or mix with pasta or fill a whole-wheat tortilla with roasted vegetables for a complete meal.

Makes 7 servings. Each 1-cup serving: 150 calories; 230 mg sodium; 0 mg cholesterol; 4 g fat; 27 g carbohydrate; 2 g protein; 4 g fiber.

Dr. William D. Stimack and Barbara Rolek

BRAISED FRESH LIMA BEANS

Fresh lima beans are sweet and tender, like peas straight from the pod. Many markets sell them already shelled.

1 clove garlic, minced
1/4 cup minced onion
1 teaspoon organic butter
1 teaspoon olive oil
2 pounds fresh lima beans, shelled
1/3 cup vegetable stock†
Non-iodized sea salt
Freshly ground black pepper
1 teaspoon fresh parsley, chopped
1 cup frisée or arugula, torn into bite-size pieces

- In medium skillet over medium heat, sauté garlic and onion in butter and oil. Stir in limas and sauté about 1 minute, stirring. Add vegetable stock. Bring to boil, then reduce heat to simmer. Cover and steam until limas are tender, about 10 minutes. Add salt and pepper to taste. Stir in parsley. Stir in frisée or arugula and cook and stir 1 minute more.

Makes 3 servings. Each serving: 550 calories; 227 mg sodium; 4 mg cholesterol; 4 g fat; 98 g carbohydrate; 34 g protein; 5.57 g fiber.

BEETS WITH ORANGE SAUCE

Highly nutritious, choose beets with firm,
smooth skin.

1 pound beets, cut into quarters
1 can organic mandarin oranges, drained with juice
   reserved
1 teaspoon arrowroot*
1 teaspoon minced fresh ginger
1 head bibb lettuce, torn into strips

- Place beets in 12" skillet and cover with water. Over high heat, bring to a boil; reduce heat, cover and simmer 30 to 35 minutes or until tender. Drain beets, remove skins; place in a serving dish and toss with lettuce.
- In small saucepan, combine reserved mandarin orange juice, arrowroot and ginger. Bring to a boil; boil 1 minute or until slightly thickened. Pour sauce over beets and lettuce, and top with mandarin oranges.

Makes 4 servings. Each serving: 82 calories; 56 mg sodium; 0 mg cholesterol; 1 g fat; 20 g carbohydrate; 1 g protein.

Dr. William D. Stimack and Barbara Rolek

SUGAR SNAP PEAS AND PEPPERS

Crisp sugar snap peas mix with red and yellow peppers for a beautiful look on the plate.

1 pound sugar snap peas, stems and strings removed
1/2 yellow bell pepper, julienned
1/2 red bell pepper, julienned
1 tablespoon olive oil
1/2 cup whole pecans
2 tablespoons chopped fresh chervil or 2 teaspoons dried
1/4 teaspoon non-iodized sea salt
1/8 teaspoon black pepper

- In a skillet, bring 1" water to boil. Add snap peas and peppers; reduce heat, cover and simmer until vegetables are crisp-tender, about 3 minutes. Drain, place in serving dish and keep warm.
- In same skillet over medium-high heat, add oil, pecans, chervil, salt and pepper, toasting lightly. Pour over the vegetables, tossing to coat.

Makes 4 servings. Each serving: 217 calories; 190 mg sodium; 5 mg cholesterol; 5 mg fat; 19 g carbohydrate; 4 g protein.

TOSSED CHARD AND BEANS

Swiss chard is a good source of vitamins A and C and iron.

1 pound Swiss chard, stalks removed
2 tablespoons canola oil
1 medium red onion, cut into rings
1 clove garlic, minced
2 tablespoons apple cider vinegar
2 tablespoons chopped fresh basil or 2 teaspoons dried
1 tablespoon honey
1 teaspoon Dijon mustard
1/4 teaspoon non-iodized sea salt
1/8 teaspoon black pepper
1 (15-ounce) can organic white kidney beans, drained

- In large skillet, bring 1" water to a boil. Add chard; cook about 5 minutes, turning once. Drain; place in serving bowl.
- In same skillet, heat oil. Sauté onion and garlic about 2 minutes. Add remaining ingredients; heat 1 minute. Spoon over chard.

Makes 4 servings. Each serving: 170 calories; 643 mg sodium; 0 mg cholesterol; 8 g fat; 28 g carbohydrate; 9 g protein.

SPINACH-ARTICHOKE BAKE

1 (6-ounce) jar marinated artichoke hearts, drained
1 (10-ounce) package frozen chopped spinach, thawed
2 green onions, chopped
8 ounces soy cream cheese,* softened
2 tablespoons olive oil
1/4 cup soy or rice milk*
2 garlic cloves, minced
1/2 teaspoon non-iodized sea salt
1/4 teaspoon Italian seasoning
1/3 cup parmesan-flavored soy topping
Tomato slices and fresh chopped parsley for garnish

- Preheat oven to 350 F. Coarsely chop artichokes and place in 8" square pan which has been lightly coated with olive oil. Squeeze spinach dry; place on top of artichokes. Top with onion. In small mixing bowl, beat cream cheese and oil until blended. Beat in milk, garlic, salt and seasoning; spread over onions. Sprinkle with parmesan topping. Cover and bake for 30 minutes. Uncover and bake 10 minutes more. Garnish with tomatoes and parsley and serve.

Makes 6 servings. Each serving: 115 Calories; 840 mg sodium; 0 mg cholesterol; 6.2 g fat; 9.2 g carbohydrate; 5.8 g protein; 2.2 g fiber.

SPAGHETTI SQUASH AU GRATIN

1 pound spaghetti squash
1 1/2 teaspoons olive oil
1/4 cup onion, chopped
1 clove garlic, minced
1 tablespoon chopped fresh basil
1/4 teaspoon freshly ground black pepper
2 tablespoons parmesan-flavored soy cheese
Non-iodized sea salt, if necessary

- Cut squash into quarters and scrape out seeds. Place 2" of water in a steamer and bring to a boil. Place squash, skin side up, in basket and lower into pot. Cover and steam for 20 minutes or till squash shreds easily. Remove and allow to cool. With a raking motion, drag fork across squash to loosen strands, and place in large bowl.
- Meanwhile, heat oil in medium skillet. Cook onion and garlic until soft, about 6 minutes. Add to squash with basil, pepper and salt, if necessary. Toss well. Place mixture in oiled baking dish. Sprinkle with soy cheese. Broil for 2 minutes and serve.

Makes 4 servings. Each serving: 50 calories; 595 mg sodium; 0 mg cholesterol; 2 g fat; 6 g carbohydrate; 1.9 g protein; 2.4 g fiber.

Dr. William D. Stimack and Barbara Rolek

CAKES, PIES
AND
OTHER GOODIES

Dr. William D. Stimack and Barbara Rolek

PIE CRUST

1 cup whole-wheat pastry flour*
3/4 teaspoon non-iodized sea salt
1/3 cup barley malt syrup* or corn syrup
2 tablespoons soy or rice milk

• In a small bowl, mix flour and salt. In another small bowl, combine barley malt syrup and milk. Add to flour mixture. Stir with a fork until thoroughly mixed. Don't overwork the dough.
• Shape mixture into a ball and place on flour-dusted surface or between two pieces of parchment paper. Roll pastry into a circle large enough to fit into a 9" pie pan. Oil pan lightly. Arrange crust in pan. Flute edges and prick bottom with a fork (if this is to be baked without a filling). Bake 10 minutes at 475 F. or until golden brown. Cool before adding filling.

Makes one 9" pie crust. Each 1/8 serving: 99 calories; 239 mg sodium; 0 mg cholesterol; 0.4 g fat; 21.5 g carbohydrate; 2.2 g protein; 1.8 g fiber.

GRAHAM CRACKER CRUST

1 1/2 cups crushed whole-wheat graham crackers
2 tablespoons date sugar* or turbinado sugar*
1 1/2 tablespoons unsweetened applesauce

- Crush graham crackers by placing in a plastic bag and rolling a pin over them. In a bowl, combined crushed crackers, sugar and applesauce. Mix well with a fork. Press into a 9" pie pan which has been lightly coated with oil. Bake at 350 F. for 10 minutes or until golden.

Makes one 9" graham cracker crust. Each 1/8 serving: 80 calories; 95 mg sodium; 0 mg cholesterol; 1.6 g fat; 15.5 g carbohydrate; 1.1 g protein; 0.4 g fiber.

PUMPKIN PIE

1 cup vanilla soy or rice milk*
2 large organic eggs, lightly beaten
1 (16-ounce) can organic unsweetened canned pumpkin
1/2 cup pure maple syrup
1 teaspoon cinnamon
1/4 teaspoon ground ginger
1/2 teaspoon nutmeg
1/2 teaspoon allspice
1/2 teaspoon non-iodized sea salt
1 unbaked 9" pie crust†

- Preheat oven to 425 F. Mix all ingredients and pour into unbaked pie crust. Bake for 15 minutes, reduce heat to 350 F. and bake for additional 40 to 50 minutes or until knife comes out clean. Remove from oven and set on wire rack to cool.

Makes 8 servings. Each serving: 202 calories; 411 mg sodium; 53 mg cholesterol; 2.4 g fat; 40.1 g carbohydrate; 5.1 g protein; 3.8 g fiber.

APPLE PIE

Try this recipe using fresh peaches, pears, strawberries, rhubarb, blueberries or pineapple in place of apples.

2 unbaked 9" pie crusts†
8 medium Granny Smith apples, peeled, cored and sliced
1 tablespoon lemon juice
1/3 cup plus 1 tablespoon turbinado sugar*
3 tablespoons spelt flour*
1/2 teaspoon cinnamon
1/4 teaspoon nutmeg
2 tablespoons organic butter
1 organic egg, beaten

- Preheat oven to 350 F. Mix apples with lemon juice. Add sugar, flour, and spices and mix again. Fit bottom crust into 9" pie pan. Fill with apple mixture and dot with butter. Place top crust on, flute edges, cut a steam hole in center, brush with beaten egg and sprinkle with sugar. Bake 1 hour or until juices bubble. Cool on wire rack.

Makes 8 servings. Each serving: 382 calories; 486 mg sodium; 35 mg cholesterol; 4.8 g fat; 78.5 g carbohydrate; 5.8 g protein; 6.6 g fiber.

"PEANUT" BUTTER PIE

1 baked graham-cracker crust†
1 pound soft tofu, drained
3/4 cup soynut butter*
1/2 cup honey
1/4 cup canola oil
1 teaspoon pure vanilla
1/8 teaspoon non-iodized sea salt

- Blend all filling ingredients in food processor until smooth and creamy. Pour into baked, cooled graham cracker crust. Decorate with sweetened carob chips,* if desired. Freeze. Let thaw for about 10 minutes before serving.

Makes 10 servings. Each serving: 332 calories; 373 mg sodium; 0 mg cholesterol; 13.7 g fat; 42.9 g carbohydrate; 9.3 g protein; 2.4 g fiber.

NEW YORK CHEESECAKE

*You CAN have your tofu cheesecake
and eat it, too!*

1 prepared graham-cracker crust†
1 1/2 pounds soft tofu
1 cup date sugar*
8 ounces soy cream cheese*
1 teaspoon pure vanilla
Pinch of non-iodized sea salt

- Preheat oven to 375 F. In a blender or food processor, purée tofu until smooth. Add sugar, soy cream cheese and vanilla, processing until smooth. Pour mixture into prepared crust and bake 50 minutes.
- Turn off heat, leaving cake in oven for 1 hour. Remove and cool. Refrigerate overnight. Serve at room temperature.

Makes 12 slices. Each slice: 170 calories; 276 mg sodium; 0 mg cholesterol; 3.28 g fat; 31.1 g carbohydrate; 4.48 g protein; 0.42.

PEACH CRISP

8 cups sliced fresh peaches
1 1/2 cups unsweetened peach juice
1/4 to 1 teaspoon white stevia* powder
2 tablespoons arrowroot*
2 cups old-fashioned rolled oats*
1/4 teaspoon ground ginger
1 teaspoon turbinado sugar*
1 tablespoon organic butter, melted

- Preheat oven to 350 F. Combine peach juice, arrowroot and stevia in a small saucepan and cook until slightly thickened. Meanwhile, place peaches in a 9"x13" glass baking dish. Mix rolled oats with ginger and sugar. Pour thickened juices over peaches and top with rolled oats mixture. Drizzle melted butter over oats. Bake 35 minutes or until bubbly.

Makes 8 servings. Each serving: 273 calories; 16 mg sodium; 4 mg cholesterol; 4.4 g fat; 50.3 g carbohydrate; 8.2 g protein; 7.6 g fiber.

Note: This can be varied by using just about any fruit. For apple, use apple juice and 1/2 teaspoon ground cinnamon in place of the ginger. Before topping with rolled oats, place 1/2 cup chopped walnuts or pecans over the apples.

For a richer dessert, top each serving with a scoop of Frozen Vanilla Rice Dream (a non-dairy alternative to ice cream available in the frozen health-food section of most stores).

APPLE CAKE

2 1/2 cups apples, peeled, cored and thinly sliced
3/4 cup turbinado sugar*
Grated rind and juice of one lemon
1 tablespoon white spelt flour*
5 tablespoons organic butter, melted
1/2 cup white spelt flour*
1/2 cup whole-wheat spelt flour*
1 teaspoon low-sodium, aluminum-free baking powder
Pinch of non-iodized sea salt
2 organic eggs
1/4 cup soy or rice milk*

- Preheat oven to 350 F. Place parchment circle on bottom of a 9" cake pan. Arrange apples in an attractive pattern in pan (when cake is done, it will be inverted onto a plate). Sprinkle apples with 1/2 cup sugar, lemon juice and rind. Cinnamon may be sprinkled on, if desired. Dust with 1 tablespoon flour and pour 4 tablespoons melted butter over apples.
- In a bowl, combine both spelt flours, remaining 1/4 cup sugar, baking powder and salt. In another bowl, beat eggs until light and quickly stir in remaining tablespoon of melted butter and the milk. Add liquid ingredients to dry, blending with as few strokes as possible. Pour batter over apples.
- Bake 30 to 40 minutes or until golden brown and toothpick comes out clean. Cover with serving platter and invert. Serve warm or at room temperature.

Makes 8 servings.   Each serving: 241 calories; 92 mg sodium; 72 mg cholesterol; 8.9 g fat; 36 g carbohydrate; 4.1 g protein; 2.7 g fiber.

Dr. William D. Stimack and Barbara Rolek

CARROT CAKE WITH ORANGE GLAZE

This cake is chock-full of carrots, raisins and nuts.

1 cup chopped walnuts
3 1/2 cups whole-wheat pastry flour*
1 teaspoon non-iodized sea salt
1 teaspoon cinnamon
1 tablespoon low-sodium, aluminum-free baking powder
1/2 cup canola oil
1/2 cup applesauce
1/2 cup apple juice
2 cups pure maple syrup
4 carrots, peeled and grated
2 tablespoons grated fresh gingerroot
1 cup chopped golden raisins

- Preheat oven to 350 F. Spread nuts on cookie sheet and toast for 10 minutes or until light brown. Cool slightly, chop and set aside.
- Sift dry ingredients together. In a separate bowl, combine liquid ingredients and add them to the dry ones. Add carrots, ginger and raisins. Mix just until well moistened. Line two 9" cake pans with parchment circles. Pour batter into pans and bake for 30 to 40 minutes, or until toothpick comes out clean. Set aside to cool.

Glaze:

Grated rind of 3 oranges
2 cups apple juice
Pinch of non-iodized sea salt
2 tablespoons arrowroot* dissolved in 1/2 cup steam-
distilled water

• Combine orange rind, apple juice and salt in a saucepan and
bring to a simmer. Stir arrowroot-water combination into
the simmering liquid. Cook, stirring, until mixture is thick.
Set aside to cool. Spread glaze over one layer. Place second
layer on top, spread remaining glaze over it and sprinkle
with chopped nuts, if desired.

Makes 12 servings. Each serving: 508 calories; 215 mg
sodium; 0 mg cholesterol; 16.2 g fat; 83.4 g carbohydrate; 7 g
protein; 6.1 g fiber.

RICE PUDDING

This is great for dessert or as a nutritious breakfast!

1 cup sweet brown (mochi) rice*
1 1/2 cups steam-distilled water
Pinch non-iodized sea salt
1 cinnamon stick
2 cups vanilla soy or rice milk*
1/4 cup raisins
1 1/2 teaspoons cinnamon
Pinch cardamom and nutmeg
Slivered, toasted almonds for garnish

- Bring to a boil rice, water, salt and cinnamon stick; cover and simmer on very low heat until water is absorbed (about 30 minutes). Add milk, raisins and spices and simmer on low, stirring frequently, until rice is soft and gooey. Remove cinnamon stick; portion out. Top with almonds and additional milk, if desired.

Makes 4 servings. Each serving: 287 calories; 20 mg sodium; 0 mg cholesterol; 6.2 g fat; 49.8 g carbohydrate; 8.2 g protein; 4.1 g fiber.

Note: For a sweeter pudding, add 2 tablespoons pure maple syrup when adding milk.

BAKED CUSTARD

2 cups soy milk*
1/4 cup honey
1/8 teaspoon non-iodized sea salt
2 organic eggs
1 teaspoon pure vanilla
Cinnamon or nutmeg for garnish

- Preheat oven to 300 F. In a bowl, combine milk, honey and salt. Add eggs and mix thoroughly. Pour mixture into custard cups or in a single baking dish. Place cups in water bath and bake for 20 minutes. Insert knife between edge of custard and cup. Custard is ready when knife comes out clean. When cool, dust with cinnamon or nutmeg.

Makes 4 servings. Each serving: 150 calories; 121 mg sodium; 105 mg cholesterol; 4.8 g fat; 20.1 g carbohydrate; 6.6 g protein; 1.6 g fiber.

CAROB BROWNIES

4 ounces organic unsalted butter
1/4 cup honey
1/4 cup pure maple syrup
1 teaspoon pure vanilla
1/3 cup unsweetened carob powder
1 cup carob soy milk*
2 1/2 cups whole-wheat pastry flour
1/4 teaspoon low-sodium, aluminum-free baking powder
1/4 cup chopped walnuts

- Preheat oven to 325 F. Melt butter in saucepan and add honey, syrup, vanilla and carob powder. Remove from heat and stir in milk. Sift together flour and baking powder. Stir into liquid mixture. Do not overmix. Fold in nuts. Spread batter into parchment-lined 8" pan. Bake for 35 minutes. Cool on wire rack before cutting.

Makes 8 servings. Each serving: 353 calories; 125 mg sodium; 31 mg cholesterol; 15.6 g fat; 46.3 g carbohydrate; 7.2 g protein; 6.4 g fiber.

CAROB-RASPBERRY CAKE
WITH ALMOND GLAZE

This company cake will please your
most discriminating guests.

Dry Ingredients:

3 cups organic white pastry flour, sifted
1 1/2 cups whole-wheat pastry flour, sifted
1 cup white spelt flour, sifted
1/2 cup unsweetened carob powder*
3 tablespoons low-sodium, aluminum-free baking
    powder

Wet Ingredients:

2 1/4 cups carob soy or rice milk
3/4 cup canola oil
3/4 cup pure maple syrup
1 1/2 cups apple juice
1 teaspoon pure vanilla
1 jar raspberry all-fruit spread

Glaze:

1 cup vanilla soy or rice milk
1 tablespoon arrowroot*
1/2 teaspoon almond extract

Almond Cream:

> 9 ounces soft tofu, blanched
> 4 tablespoons pure maple syrup
> 1/4 teaspoon almond extract

- Preheat oven to 350 F. Place parchment circles in two 9" cake pans. Combine all dry ingredients in a large bowl. In a separate bowl, combine wet ingredients (except for raspberry all-fruit spread). Slowly add wet ingredients to dry until combined. Divide batter evenly between cake pans. Bake until toothpick comes out clean, about 25 to 30 minutes. When cake has cooled, remove from pans and spread with raspberry all-fruit over each cake and layer one on top of the other.
- For glaze: Mix arrowroot, vanilla milk and almond extract in a saucepan over medium heat, until thickened. Pour over cake.
- For almond cream: Blend tofu with maple syrup and almond extract in blender until smooth and creamy. Dollop onto cake when ready to serve and garnish with raspberries and slivered almonds.

Makes 12 servings. Each serving without almond cream: 500 calories; 57 mg sodium; 0 mg cholesterol; 15 g fat; 86 g carbohydrate; 10 g protein; 6 g fiber.

CANTALOUPE SORBET

1 large ripe cantaloupe (about 2 1/2 pounds)
1/2 cup fresh orange juice
2 teaspoons grated lemon peel or 1/2 teaspoon lemon
    extract
1 tablespoon honey
1/2 cup green seedless grapes, for garnish
Cantaloupe triangles, for garnish

- Cut cantaloupe into chunks and place in food processor fitted with steel blade; process. You should have 2 1/2 cups purée. Add orange juice and lemon peel or extract; process to blend. Taste; add honey if mixture is not sweet enough. Freeze in ice-cream maker according to manufacturer's instructions.
- At serving time, divide grapes among 4 parfait glasses; place scoop of sorbet over grapes; decorate with cantaloupe triangles. Serve immediately.

Makes 4 servings. Each serving: 144 calories; 28 mg sodium; 0 mg cholesterol; 1 g fat; 35 g carbohydrate; 3 g protein; 3 g fiber.

Dr. William D. Stimack and Barbara Rolek

"CHOCOLATE" SYRUP

*You'll dream up thousands of uses
for this dessert sauce.*

3 tablespoons vanilla soy or rice milk*
4 tablespoons unsweetened carob powder*
2 tablespoons almond butter*
5 tablespoons pure maple syrup

- Place all ingredients in blender and process until smooth. Store in refrigerator. Use as a dessert topping or to make chocolate milk.

Makes 1/2 cup. Each tablespoon: 73 calories; 21 mg sodium; 0 mg cholesterol; 2.8 g fat; 10.8 g carbohydrate; 1.3 g protein; 1.1 g fiber.

COOKIES

Dr. William D. Stimack and Barbara Rolek

BASIC COOKIE DOUGH

Let your imagination run wild
as you turn this basic dough into all sorts of cookies.

    1 cup walnuts (6 ounces)
    2 cups old-fashioned rolled oats*
    1/2 cup rice flour*
    1/4 teaspoon non-iodized sea salt
    1/2 teaspoon ground cinnamon
    1/4 teaspoon ground allspice
    1/4 teaspoon freshly grated or ground nutmeg
    1/4 cup canola oil
    1/3 cup brown rice syrup*
    1/3 cup pure maple syrup
    1 tablespoon pure vanilla
    3 tablespoons all-fruit spread

- Preheat oven to 350 F. Toast walnuts 8 to 10 minutes. Line 3 baking sheets with parchment paper; set aside.
- Meanwhile, put oats in food processor and pulse on/off 6 times. Add rice flour, salt and spices, and pulse. Scrape down sides and pulse 2 more times to thoroughly combine. Transfer to large bowl.
- While walnuts are still warm, grind them to a paste in food processor. Add oil, rice syrup, maple syrup and vanilla, and process until blended and smooth. Add to dry ingredients and mix until just well blended (dough will be sticky).
- Scoop out heaping teaspoonfuls of dough and roll into balls. Place on baking sheets and flatten to form cookies about 1 3/4"

in diameter, spaced 2" apart. (It's helpful to dip hands and utensils in cold water when working with this sticky dough.)
* With your thumb, make a deep indentation in center of each cookie. Fill each with about 1/4 teaspoon fruit spread. Bake until bottoms are lightly browned, about 20 minutes. Transfer cookies to wire racks to cool.

Note: Different fillings can be used for this cookie or you may top them with a slivered almond or finely chopped nuts. This dough can also be rolled between two sheets of parchment paper to 1/8" thickness, cut with cookie cutters and baked for 8 minutes.

Makes 3 dozen cookies. Each cookie: 90 calories; 20 mg sodium; 0 mg cholesterol; 5 g fat; 11 g carbohydrate; 2 g protein; 1 g fiber.

APRICOT POPPYSEED COOKIES

Company cookies that are low in fat
and high in flavor.

1/2 cup poppyseeds
1 cup almonds (6 ounces)
2 cups old-fashioned rolled oats*
1 1/2 cups rice flour*
1/4 teaspoon non-iodized sea salt
1 teaspoon ground cinnamon
1/2 teaspoon ground cardamom
1/3 cup canola oil
1/2 cup brown rice syrup*
1 cup apricot all-fruit spread
1 teaspoon almond extract
1/3 cup blanched, slivered almonds

- Preheat oven to 350 F. In small skillet, toast poppyseeds over medium-high heat, stirring often until they change color slightly, 2 to 3 minutes; set aside. Place almonds on baking sheet and toast lightly, 8 to 10 minutes. Line 2 baking sheets with parchment paper; set aside.
- In food processor, finely grind toasted almonds, oats and flour. Transfer to large bowl. Add poppyseeds, salt, spices and mix well.
- In medium bowl, mix oil, rice syrup, apricot spread and almond extract until blended. Add to dry ingredients and mix just until combined (dough will be sticky).

- Roll 1 tablespoon dough into a ball, place on baking sheet and flatten to form a cookie about 1 3/4" in diameter, spaced 1" apart. (It's helpful to dip hands and utensils in cold water when working with this sticky dough.) Press blanched, slivered almonds into centers of each cookie. Bake until bottoms are lightly browned, about 12 minutes. These cookies are very delicate; allow to cool on pans for several minutes, then remove to wire racks to cool completely.

Makes 5 dozen cookies. Each cookie: 80 calories; 15 mg sodium; 0 mg cholesterol; 4 g fat; 11 g carbohydrate; 1 g protein; 1 g fiber.

MAPLE-PECAN SANDIES

A perfect pairing of flavors.

1 cup pecans (6 ounces), plus 18 pecan halves for garnish
1 cup old-fashioned rolled oats*
1 cup rice flour*
1/4 teaspoon non-iodized sea salt
2 teaspoons ground cinnamon
1/4 teaspoon ground nutmeg
1/2 cup pure maple syrup
2 tablespoons canola oil
1 tablespoon pure vanilla

- Preheat oven to 350 F. Toast 1 cup pecans 8 to 10 minutes. Remove from oven and cool slightly.
- In food processor, finely grind toasted pecans. Add oats, flour, salt and spices. Pulse on/off several times to combine ingredients. Scrape down sides and pulse 2 more times to thoroughly combine. Transfer to large bowl.
- In medium bowl, mix syrup, oil and vanilla. Add to flour mixture and stir until well blended.
- Roll 1 tablespoon dough into a ball and place on parchment-lined baking sheet. Flatten to form cookie about 1 3/4" in diameter. Press a pecan half in center of each. Repeat with remainder of dough, spacing about 1" apart. Bake until bottoms are lightly browned, about 10 minutes. Transfer to wire racks to cool.

Makes 18 cookies. Each cookie: 160 calories; 31 mg sodium; 0 mg cholesterol; 9 g fat; 19 g carbohydrate; 2 g protein; 1 g fiber.

"CHOCOLATE" CHIPS

Mrs. Fields, look out!

1 cup whole-wheat flour*
1 cup organic unbleached white flour*
3/4 cup sweetened carob chips*
1/2 cup canola oil
1/2 cup chopped walnuts or pecans
3/4 cup pure maple syrup
1 teaspoon pure vanilla
1/2 cup soy or rice milk
1 tablespoon low-sodium, aluminum-free baking powder

- Preheat oven to 350 F. Mix all ingredients in large bowl. Drop by spoonfuls onto parchment-lined cookie sheet. Bake 10 minutes or until edges begin to brown.

Makes 3 dozen cookies. Each cookie: 124 calories; 35 mg sodium; 0 mg cholesterol; 8 g fat; 13 g carbohydrate; 2 g protein; 1 g fiber.

Dr. William D. Stimack and Barbara Rolek

"PEANUT" BUTTER COOKIES

These are not low in fat or sodium, but when peanut butter cookies call to you, this soynut version is a little healthier.

1/4 cup unsalted organic butter, softened
1/4 cup turbinado sugar*
3 organic egg whites
1 1/4 cups soynut butter*
Pinch non-iodized sea salt
1/2 teaspoon baking soda
1 teaspoon pure vanilla
1/2 cup oat flour*
1 cup spelt flour

- Preheat oven to 350 F. Cream butter and sugar till light and fluffy. Add eggs whites, soynut butter, salt, baking soda and vanilla, mixing well. Mix together flours and add to wet ingredients, blending well.
- Roll dough into balls about the size of walnuts. Place on parchment-lined cookie sheets. Flatten with fork dipped in spelt flour. Bake 7 to 9 minutes. Cool on wire racks.

Makes 2 dozen small cookies. Each cookie: 195 calories; 168 mg sodium; 5 mg cholesterol; 11.3 g fat; 15.8 g carbohydrate; 7.7 g protein; 1.6 g fiber.

ALMOND CLUSTERS

1 cup raw almonds, ground
1/2 cup brown rice syrup*
1/2 teaspoon ground cinnamon
1/2 teaspoon almond or pure vanilla extract
3 tablespoons unsalted organic butter
3 cups crushed organic cereal—oat bran flakes or your choice

- Mix all ingredients but cereal. Stir in cereal, coating well. Shape into small balls. Place on parchment-lined sheet pan and chill.

Makes 3 dozen. Each cluster: 50 calories; 30 mg sodium; 3 mg cholesterol; 2.5 g fat; 6 g carbohydrate; 0.9 g protein; 0.7 g fiber.

FRUIT AND HONEY CANDY

8 ounces each dried apricots, apples and peaches
6 ounces dried fruit bits
3/4 cup honey
1 teaspoon orange extract
1 1/2 cups old-fashioned rolled oats*
1 cup walnut pieces
3/4 cup walnut pieces, finely chopped

- In food processor with metal blade, combine dried fruits. Process 2 to 3 minutes or until fruit is finely chopped. Add honey and orange extract. Process an additional 2 to 3 minutes or until well blended.
- In small bowl, combine oats and 1 cup walnut pieces. Add to fruit mixture and process 2 minutes or until walnuts are chopped. Form mixture into balls. Roll in 3/4 cup finely chopped walnuts. Place in candy cups and store in airtight container.

Makes 7 dozen. Each candy: 61 calories; 2 mg sodium; 0 mg cholesterol; 1.6 g fat; 10.6 g carbohydrate; 0.9 g protein; 1.2 g fiber.

BEVERAGES

Dr. William D. Stimack and Barbara Rolek

GINGER TEA

A soothing hot tea with medicinal properties.

6 cups steam-distilled water
Slices of peeled, fresh ginger
Fresh lemon juice
Honey

- Boil water. Add slices of ginger and steep, covered, until the flavor of the ginger is infused throughout the water, about 8 minutes or longer if you like a stronger flavor. Remove ginger before serving.
- You may add a squeeze of fresh lemon juice and a spoonful of honey, if you desire.

Makes 6 servings.

Dr. William D. Stimack and Barbara Rolek

BANANA-STRAWBERRY SMOOTHIE

A refreshing drink anytime of the day.

1 very ripe frozen banana
1 cup strawberries
2 cups vanilla soy milk*

- Freeze very ripe bananas in their peels until solid. Remove peel and place frozen banana in blender with strawberries and vanilla soy milk. Blend until smooth and thick. If the banana is very ripe, no additional sweetener should be necessary. Stevia* may be added if a sweeter drink is desired.

Makes 4 servings. Each serving: 88 calories; 44 mg sodium; 4 mg cholesterol; 1 g fat; 17 g carbohydrate; 4 g protein; 2 g fiber.

PAPAYA POWER SHAKE

A great breakfast drink!

1 papaya (or mango), peeled, seeded and cut up
1 cup soy sour cream*
1/2 ripe banana
1/2 cup pineapple chunks
1/2 teaspoon dried mint
4 ice cubes, slightly crushed

- Combine all ingredients in a blender and whirl until smooth.

Makes 4 servings.   Each serving: 88 calories; 44 mg sodium; 4 mg cholesterol; 1 g fat; 17 g carbohydrate; 4 g protein; 2 g fiber.

TROPICAL SMOOTHIE

2 cups pineapple juice
1 banana
1 large kiwi, peeled
1/4 to 1 teaspoon green stevia powder*

- Process all ingredients in a blender until smooth.

Makes 2 servings.   Each serving: 249 calories; 4 mg sodium; 0 mg cholesterol; 0.7 g fat; 58.6 g carbohydrate; 2 g protein; 3.5 g fiber.

Dr. William D. Stimack and Barbara Rolek

STRAWBERRY SLUSH

1/2 cup very hot steam-distilled water
1/4 teaspoon white stevia powder*
1 cup ice cubes
2 pints strawberries, stemmed, rinsed and quartered
1 tablespoon fresh lime juice (or more to taste)
Sliced fresh strawberries

- Combine hot water and stevia in blender and process until stevia is dissolved. Add ice and blend until mixture is slushy. With blender running, gradually add strawberries and process until puréed. Garnish each glass with sliced strawberries.

Makes 4 servings. Each serving: 78 calories; 2 mg sodium; 0 mg cholesterol; 0.8 g fat; 16.2 g carbohydrate; 1.4 g protein; 5.2 g fiber.

MISCELLANEOUS

Dr. William D. Stimack and Barbara Rolek

EGGLESS MAYONNAISE

1 cup unflavored soy milk*
1 tablespoon onion powder
1 teaspoon non-iodized sea salt
1/4 to 1/2 teaspoon stevia* extract (white powdered)
Juice of 1 lemon
2 cups cold-pressed oil* (canola, safflower, etc.)

- Place soy milk in food processor fitted with the metal blade and add onion powder, salt, stevia and lemon juice.
- Process for about 30 seconds as you slowly add oil through the feed tube. The mixture will begin to thicken. Longer processing will result in thicker mayonnaise.

Makes 3 cups. Each tablespoon: 84 calories; 50 mg sodium; 0 mg cholesterol; 9.2 g fat; 0.2 g carbohydrate; 0.1 g protein; 0.1 g fiber.

LOW-SODIUM SEASONINGS

Try these low-sodium spice blends in your shaker instead of salt.

HERBED SEASONING

  2 tablespoons dried dillweed or basil
  2 tablespoons onion powder
  1 teaspoon dried oregano leaves, crumbled
  1 teaspoon celery seed
  1/4 teaspoon grated dried lemon peel
  Pinch of freshly ground black pepper

• Combine all ingredients in small bowl and blend well. Spoon into shaker and store in a cool, dark place.

Makes about 1/3 cup. Each teaspoon: 0.65 mg sodium.

SPICY BLEND

  2 tablespoons dried savory, crumbled
  1 tablespoon dry mustard
  1 1/2 teaspoons onion powder
  1 3/4 teaspoons curry powder
  1 1/4 teaspoons freshly ground white pepper
  1 1/4 teaspoons ground cumin
  1/2 teaspoon garlic powder

- Combine all ingredients in small bowl and blend well. Spoon into shaker and store in a cool, dark place.

Makes about 1/3 cup. Each teaspoon: 0.59 mg sodium.

NO-SALT SEASONING

1 teaspoon chili powder
2 teaspoons ground oregano
2 teaspoons black pepper
1 tablespoon garlic powder
1 tablespoon dry mustard
6 tablespoons onion powder
3 tablespoons paprika
3 tablespoons poultry seasoning

- Combine all ingredients in small bowl and blend well. Spoon into shaker and store in a cool dark place.

Makes 1 cup. 0 mg sodium.

Dr. William D. Stimack and Barbara Rolek

THYME AND ROSEMARY RUB

Try this on fish, potatoes, eggplant and tomatoes before broiling.

1 tablespoon chopped fresh rosemary or 1 teaspoon dried
1 tablespoon chopped fresh thyme or 1 teaspoon dried
1 teaspoon finely minced garlic
1/4 teaspoon non-iodized sea salt
1/4 teaspoon freshly ground black pepper

- In a small bowl, combine all ingredients. Rub this on lightly oiled fish and vegetables before broiling.

Makes 1/3 cup. Each tablespoon: 3 calories; 107 mg sodium; 0 mg cholesterol; 0 g fat; 1 g carbohydrate; 0 g protein; 0 g fiber.

CHILI SPICE PASTE

*This simple paste zips up everything from
vegetables to soups to salsas.*

1 tablespoon olive oil
1 tablespoon chili powder
1 teaspoon dried oregano
1 teaspoon dried cumin
1/4 teaspoon ground red pepper
1/8 teaspoon salt

- Combine all ingredients, mixing well. This is great for corn on the cob, broiled tomatoes, peppers and zucchini. Combine with roasted vegetables in wraps; add to chili; go wild.

Makes 2 tablespoons. Each tablespoon: 79 calories; 174 mg sodium; 0 mg cholesterol; 8 g fat; 3 g carbohydrate; 1 g protein; 1 g fiber.

BARBECUE SAUCE

8 ounces tomato sauce†
1/2 cup finely chopped onion
1/2 cup finely chopped green pepper
1/2 cup finely chopped celery
4 cloves garlic, crushed
2 tablespoons apple cider vinegar
2 tablespoons pure maple syrup
1 tablespoon Worcestershire sauce
1/4 teaspoon freshly ground black pepper (optional)
1/4 teaspoon cayenne or a few dashes of bottled hot pepper sauce

- In a small saucepan, combine all ingredients and bring to a boil. Reduce heat, cover and simmer for 15 minutes. Uncover and simmer about 10 minutes more or until of desired consistency.

Makes 1 cup. Each tablespoon: 12 calories; 18 mg sodium; 0 mg cholesterol; 0 g fat; 2.9 g carbohydrate; 0.1 g protein; 0.3 g fiber.

SAMPLE MENUS

These are meant as a guideline only.
Mix and match as you see fit, as long as you remain
within the RDAs. *

Breakfast   Creamy Oatmeal†
             1/2 banana
             1 cup soy or rice milk

Lunch   Italian Chickpeas and Rice Soup†
             1/2 whole-wheat pita
             Fruit

Dinner   Mushroom Stroganoff†
             Green, Leafy Salad
             Melon Wedges

****

Breakfast   French Toast†
             Ginger Tea†

Lunch   Veggie Bean Burger†
             Whole-wheat bun
             Tomato, Cucumber and Lettuce for sandwich
             Creamy Cilantro-Sesame Dressing† as a spread
             Fruit

Dinner   Red Pepper Tofu Frittata†

Peach Crisp†

****

Breakfast   Sweet Millet Cereal†

Lunch   Eggless Egg Salad†
Romaine Lettuce
Tomato

Dinner   Fajitas with Avocado "Sour Cream" Sauce†
Whole-wheat tortillas with romaine lettuce and
    salsa
Mango wedges with lime juice

****

Breakfast   Huevos Rancheros†

Lunch   Sloppy Joe Lentils†
Whole-wheat bun
Fruit

Dinner   Broiled Fish of Choice
Herbed Brown Rice Pilaf†
Sugar Snap Peas and Peppers†
Green, Leafy Salad
Carob Brownie†

****

Breakfast   Pancakes†

Lunch   Whole-wheat Tortilla with Roasted Vegetables†
            Fruit

Dinner   Squash Italiano†
            Green, Leafy Salad
            Whole-Wheat Bread
            Cantaloupe Sorbet†

****

Breakfast   Tempeh and Potato Sausages†
            1 organic egg

Lunch   Southwestern Potato-Corn Wrap
            Fruit

Dinner   Poached Salmon with Asparagus-Rice Pilaf†
            Green, Leafy Salad
            New York Cheesecake

****

Breakfast   Papaya Power Shake
            1 piece whole-wheat toast

Lunch   Spinach-Artichoke Bake†
            Green, Leafy Salad
            Fruit

Dinner   Mushroom Stroganoff†

259

Wild Rice†
Carrot Cake with Orange Glaze†

****

Breakfast   Morning Glory Muffin†
1 cup soy or rice milk

Lunch   "Sausage" Pizza
Green, Leafy Salad

Dinner   Broiled Cold-Water Fish of Choice
Cajun Beans and Barley†
Green, Leafy Salad
Baked Custard†

****

Breakfast   Nutri-Muffin†
1 cup soy or rice milk

Lunch   Salmon and New Potato Salad†
Fruit

Dinner   Eggplant "Parmesan"†
Green, Leafy Salad
"Peanut" Butter Pie†

SOURCE LIST

ORGANIC FOOD COOP

Blooming Prairie Natural Foods
510 Kasota Avenue SE
Minneapolis, MN 55414
(612) 378-9774
www.bpco-op.com

BREAD PRODUCTS

Natural Ovens of Manitowoc Wisconsin
P.O. Box 730
Manitowoc, WI 54221-0730
(800) 558-3535
www.naturalovens.com

FLOURS AND BAKING PRODUCTS

King Arthur® Flour
P.O. Box 876
Norwich, VT 05055
(800) 827-6836
www.BakersCatalogue.com

Hodgson Mill
1203 Niccum Ave.
Effingham, IL 62401
(800) 347-0105

www.hodgsonmill.com

SOY BURGERS, GROUND SOY AND SOY SAUSAGES

Boca Foods Company
P.O. Box 8995
Madison, WI 53708
(608) 285-6820
www.bocaburger.com

NAYONAISE SOY MAYONNAISE

Vitasoy USA Inc.
400 Oyster Point Blvd., Suite 201
South San Francisco, CA 94080
(800) 848-2769
www.vitasoy-usa.com

SOYNUT BUTTER AND OTHER NUT BUTTERS

The SoyNut Butter Company
4220 Commercial Way
Glenview, IL 60025
(800) 288-1012
www.soynutbutterco.com

VEGGIE SHREDS SOY CHEESE AND OTHER PRODUCTS

Galaxy Foods Company
2441 Viscount Row

Orlando, FL 32809
(800) 808-2325
www.veggieforlife.com

GIMME LEAN, SMART BACON AND OTHER PRODUCTS

Lightlife Foods
153 Industrial Blvd.
Turners Falls, MA 01376
www.lightlife.com

SILK SOY MILK AND OTHER PRODUCTS

White Wave, Inc.
1990 N. 57th Ct.
Boulder, CO 80301
www.whitewave.com

Eden Foods, Inc.
701 Tecumseh Road
Clinton, MI 49236
(888) 441-3336
www.edenfoods.com

Dr. William D. Stimack and Barbara Rolek

RICE DREAM PRODUCTS

Imagine Foods, Inc.
1245 San Carlos Ave.
San Carlos, CA 94070
(650) 595-6300
www.imaginefoods.com
e-mail: questions@imaginefoods.com

ORGANIC SUCANAT AND ORGANIC SUGAR

Wholesome Sweeteners
P.O. Box 339
Savannah, GA 31402
(912) 651-4820
www.wholesomesweeteners.com

ABOUT THE AUTHORS

Dr. William D. Stimack is the president and chief executive officer of Integrated Healthcare Systems Inc. located in Valparaiso, Indiana. He holds doctorates of naturopathy (N.D.) and naturopathic medicine (N.M.D.) degrees from Southern College of Naturopathy in Boles, Arkansas, whose board of trustees recently appointed him to the position of director of nutrition.

Dr. Stimack is also a certified practitioner of herbology, acupuncture, Chinese and homeopathic medicine, is licensed by the District of Columbia and the State of North Carolina, and has applied for licensure in the State of Kentucky. At this time, the State of Indiana does not have a naturopathic licensing requirement.

He is a member of the American Naturopathic Medical Association, certified and accredited by the American Association of Drugless Practitioners, and board-certified by the American Naturopathic Medical Certification and Accreditation Board.

At least twice a year, Dr. Stimack donates his time and medicines to work with the underprivileged at a free clinic in Moribosco, Mexico.

Dr. Stimack lives with his wife, Jean, in Valparaiso.

Barbara Rolek is a former executive chef and culinary-school instructor living in Crown Point, Indiana, where she is a lifestyle features writer specializing in health and nutrition. In addition to writing a weekly newspaper column, "Food for Thought," Ms. Rolek reviews restaurants in the Chicago Metropolitan and Northwest Indiana areas.

She writes for *Epicurean Traveler* and *Midwest Living* magazines and on-line for *cheftalk.com*. Ms. Rolek is currently working on a book of healthy gourmet recipes, a culinary mystery and a cooking memoir.

Please direct your comments or inquiries to:

Dr. William D. Stimack
P.O. Box 1366
Valparaiso, IN 46383

If you prefer to communicate via e-mail, you may contact the authors at:

bjrolek@netnitco.net

Printed in the United States
3787

9 780759 682139